PARIS ALWAYS PARIS

Paris Always Paris

Nilda Cepero

House of the Tragic Poet

Other books by Nilda Cepero:

Poetry
Sugar Cane Blues
Lil' Havana Blues
A Blues Cantata
Bohemian Canticles
Hemingway, The Last Daiquiri
Short Stories
Más Allá del Azul
Memoirs
Recuerdos de Sevilla y otros caminos
A mi gusto: La cocina de las "muchachitas"
    To my Liking: The Cuisine of the "Girls"
    (bilingual)

Front cover: *Night at Pont Royal. Paris.* By the Author
Back cover: *Pont Royal in Pink. Paris.* By the Author

To protect the privacy of certain individuals, the names and identifying details have been changed.

"All the world's a stage
And all the men and women merely players:
They have their exits and their entrances;
And one man in his time plays many parts"
—William Shakespeare
[As You Like It, Act II, Scene VII]

For those family members who have always stayed by my side — even through my painful, creative years. Poor guys! [pobrecitos]. I'll forever remember you fondly.

To E J, for being so special: "Night and Day, you are the one..."

The last few days of a very dry winter in South Florida were quickly turning moist, as we finished a meeting at the French Alliance in Miami. I was excited. The Board had approved my proposal for an exhibition of my work. They figured I could put into practice my years of experience and share the photographs of my Paris adventures.

"Why not?", Madame Ferré said. "As soon as you return from Paris let's organize it. You can do a one-woman show with all the bells and whistles. *Oui, oui oui*, by all means, let's do it!".

It happened so fast I didn't realize we had romanticized the whole idea and putting it into practice was going to require a lot of organizing, hard work and patience. Still, what the heck, it was the city of love. France, especially Paris, has unparalleled magnetism. As the main ingredient, all you have to do is add wine and cheese to a table by the roadside: *et te voilá mon ami.*

From the beginning. Forever restless, years ago my mother bought me a camera to help me burn some energy. Eagerly, my senses showed so much interest in art composition, that she seized the moment and took me to meet her friends, Berta Randín and Enrique Riverón. The old Cuban masters praised my new activity and recommended I should also experiment with painting. I did, and learned a lot from them, especially about color. I also entered some photographic competitions at an art academy, and found the displays stimulating. Because of my love for butterflies on account of the color they radiate, my submissions included those colorful insects.

Considering that actions we take are always linked to other unexpected designs, while visiting Butterfly World in South Florida, a large poster of the Tuileries Garden showed up in the background of one of the displays. Fascinated by the sight, I left the camera hanging from my neck and stared at the banner: tulips, roses, jasmines, and the palace in the background. The images claimed me. Transfixed, I stood looking at it for a few minutes. It was unmitigated joy and peace.

Prior to moving to my next *papillon*, I made my decision: Paris would be my next assignment. Although I'm a poet at heart and spend most of my time expressing perceptual sensitivity, it is also important to stimulate other artistic curiosities. I knew that with photography, like with any other endeavor, an individual needs an exciting place to get inspired, where ideas could be stirred up. And what better site to spark it than the City of Light?

Weeks later, the images each student put together were fascinating. And my photographs, with butterflies fluttering with castles in the background, were a success. That is how my interest in photography was triggered. I even wrote a few poems to add to the art catalog.

Step by step. During high school in Boston, it was luck what prompted me to meet a rookie teacher who had spent time in Europe. She encouraged me to take French history and art history at the local Junior College. This young woman inspired me to learn about kings and their *maîtresse-en-titre* [official mistress], the Revolution, the French Renaissance and the painters from different periods. And I did. All of it riveting, and my love affair with Paris flourished.

I learned painters were inspired by the luminosity of Paris. Locals like Manet, Renoir, Monet, Degas, Seurat, Gauguin, and Rousseau, and foreigners like Picasso, Dalí and Miró. Moreover, it just happened that in literature we also covered the American writers who lived there during the interwar period. Their fiction, poetry and memoirs touched me deeply. Defined by Gertrude Stein as "the lost generation", there at the helm of the group was a young, good looking and dynamic Ernest Hemingway, who as a doughboy had fallen in love with Europe, and especially

10

Paris. It captivated him. It was in Paris where he arrived in 1921 with his first wife, Hadley, and departed with his second one, the wealthy Pauline Pfeiffer, in 1928. If the wily Hem wanted to write with ease and no financial worries, he figured the switch would work to his advantage.

In my senior year of high school, with the help of an enthusiastic music teacher, Ms. LeCouffe, a French Quebecois, a scholarship to spend my spring term in France became a reality. Excited, I began to look for group travel deals. While counting my pennies from part-time jobs, the perfect fit came up: An educational tour was forming and a few of my fellow students also joined.

Teeming with optimism and fresh ideas, I went to every French film festival that could be found. The flickering images on the screen, the romantic dialog and the French accent sent quivering waves up my spine.

This trip, among others to come later, eventually delineated the blueprint to follow: To capture images of Paris the way I conceived her to be. In a way, my story of the city became a lifetime project for its continuity. The yarns wrote themselves in my journals about the metropolis; something of a habit of mine.

Comparing myself to others, the one trait exceedingly obvious is the romantic in me. It is displayed in my poetry as well as in my prose, it is, moreover, the essence that thrusts me to adventure. However, no matter how dreamy or whimsical one could get, like in a chemical reaction, there has to be a catalyst to provide the spark. Workshops, books and films do provide impetus, but there has to be persuasion. My godmother, Hortensia, called "introduction to culture" everything she saw me doing. The scholarship trip sealed my future sojourns to Paris.

In my teens, long before the Paris trip, I went sightseeing with my parents around the country. The north of Mexico, even. Also Quebec City—an Old World variety citadel—the Maritimes, and the colorful bayous of New Orleans, but never across the Atlantic. What I remember most fondly about US cities is their food and how American, but different, they were.

Aside from traveling, my mother and I also enjoyed old romantic films, especially those with French themes or locations. The storylines were beguiling and, consequently, galvanized my curiosity. On one occasion, after exiting the theater, mom promised we would visit Paris someday: "If only I could convince your father to hop on a plane and cross the ocean."

Impacted by the images on the screen, I often day-dreamed of walking by the Seine, just like the heroine *du jour*. Mimicking the scenes and dialogs, I felt unique sensations, and the stimuli told me that, for certain, I would find myself someday in its milieu.

Because I've always enjoyed writing, long ago, encouraged by my mother, I began to keep a journal of my travels. Moreover, entrusted now to bring Paris in photographs to the French Alliance of Miami, I said to myself: Why not add to my expo all the logs I scribbled and make it into a memoir? First stop, the travel journals.

Study Abroad Program. My first personal experience with Paris was supposed to be an introduction to the metropolis itself, to its art, and to immerse into a new culture; however, it became more like a revelation analogous to an epiphany.

In my head I was ready to take a million pics to share. I packed my camera, a dictionary, books, language tapes and, of course, maps. I had learned about the twenty arrondissements and contemplated strolling through gardens, across bridges, and parks. Never, in my most vivid imagining, did I think I would make lasting friendships and become a Francophile. As the departure date approached, and my excitement was at its apex, things began to crumble. The dark clouds included the flu, break-ups and even a funeral. Moreover, my parents were now apprehensive about the dangers I could face by traveling alone. In any event, as an impatient rebel, I did not relent.

Holding back tears, I reached for the phone and called my generous and wise godmother, Hortensia. On the call, she was emphatic and clear: *"Avanti!"*, she roared, "tell your parents that I will accompany you."

Hortensia. She was a hodophile, my benefactor, and well-wisher extraordinaire who loved my singing. Every time she dropped by I vivaciously played the piano and, being a ham, always put on a show for her.

Hortensia journeyed to Europe every year to see her family in Spain, but would visit Paris first, always. According to her, the Louvre deserved a visit every time. She prided herself on being an art enthusiast and knew all about artists and their work. From her I heard, for the first time, about Picasso, Valázquez, Goya, Monet, Manet, Renoir, and many others. And, by the time I was taking art classes, there was now a stronger connection between us.

She was a skillful raconteur and I'm convinced her stories became the seed that nurtured my imagination. On her many returns from Europe, she always brought me postcards, intoxicating chocolates, and perfumes. Once she presented me with an elegant French doll I still have.

She didn't have children, but, at some point, had enjoyed the bliss of marriage. Always telling my mother how she would have loved a daughter to show her the world.

Hortensia was an inspiration to all who knew her. Learning much from her ways, her remarks came in handy later on when I needed to make a good impression.

I can still visualize how she dressed in an elegant, polished style. Always carried herself in a suave way that reflected her upbringing. Her mother was a classical pianist and her father taught philosophy. Because she was refined and stylish, it gave me a heightened awareness of how to be feminine, and taught me that it was never old-fashioned to wear classic styles. "Never follow trends", she reminded me. Oh, yes, I remember her fondly and the stories she shared. If Hortensia only knew the impact her narratives and gifts—especially the perfumes—had on me! Whenever I sprayed them on, I felt rapture. As if holy water, upon touching the skin, had turned my soul pure.

Now that Hortensia decided to join me, the whole scene mellowed out and my family turned optimistic once again.

While making plans, I mentioned to Hortensia I was supposed to lodge in a dorm. However, she would hear none of it. "I'll take care of it. That's my domain." And with a phone call she made reservations at the Sevigne hotel [today Hotel Emily at rue 2 Malher in the Marais], a quiet and graceful place on a short road off rue de Rivoli, near Saint-Paul metro; a safe and delightful family-oriented neighborhood. I was excited as any teenager would be.

A week before parting, my mother was told cousin Gloria from Spain would also be in Paris in the spring taking French lessons. I was elated. Now I had someone else I knew to see the sights.

Mon année de pèlerinage. Spring travel always delivers rain. A downpour leaving the States, a light shower landing in Paris. The flight itself was uneventful, as I slept most of the way. Arriving while the city was rising, we picked up our luggage and took a cab. Getting to the city was a rousing experience. Hortensia laughed and said, "you remind me of a little puppy looking out the window."

The cab driver careened in and out of traffic very rapidly. It was a lovely flourishing day as we entered the city proper, with the clouds moving on.

Quick images of the surroundings flickered through the window, and, to my surprise, Paris was greeting me and unearthing unaware emotions that were now part of my psyche. I suppose they had been there all along from the moment I immersed myself in the French way of life. Taking in the scenery made me recall those wonderful films about Paris I had enjoyed with my mother in gentler times.

The hotel was exactly like the pictures in the travel brochure. Small, charming, very safe, and, to a general extent, within a walking distance of many museums, including Picasso's, Place des Vosges, and other sights that were important to Hortensia. We were, as well, near enough to the charming *Île Saint Louis*, where many other famous buildings are located. Also beautiful stores everywhere and, of course, the Seine.

That morning, breakfast was still being served and brought to the room. Croissants, jelly, cheese and the tea and coffee they had available. It was appetizing. After finishing the meal, I opened the door to the balcony and a soft breeze entered the room. I stepped outside and breathed the fresh morning air.

With impressive wrought iron balustrades, the buildings in the neighborhood reminded me of postcards I had seen of facades in Seville, Barcelona, New Orleans and Old Havana, but didn't know Paris also had them. Looking at the busy street below, I was smitten by the panorama. And I asked myself if one has to be in love to let Paris love us.

Stepping back into the room, I then settled down to take a nap and so did Hortensia, who had been sorting out her clothes. But it was hard to unwind. The excitement that awaited me in the days to come made me toss and turn, and I said to myself: I should not waste my time in bed while the city was ready to be enjoyed.

On this trip with my godmother, the thought crossing my mind was open-eyed fun while she was with me, including visiting some of the sights important to her and also the marvelous stores filled with the sweet scents she always talked about. It was likewise marvelous that she spoke French — with a refreshing Spanish accent. Once on her way to Spain and with my agenda beginning, I knew my visit would turn into a deeper cultural experience and have a more liberating aim.

Hortensia's plan was for her to be with me for two weeks to help me settle down and find me a small apartment to stay — she insisted on paying for everything — and, after showing me some of the sights, go back home via Madrid. Her heart was set and she had a list to prove it. We took taxis everywhere we could.

Nevertheless, I spoke to Gloria and we decided that, once Hortensia left Paris, I would be welcome to also stay at her friend's place. It was in the Marais near everything, although it was rather small. Still and all, on this I bypassed godmother and kept her out of the loop. She had her heart set on doing everything for me like a hovering parent, and the "list" she had for me was intimidating.

The tour begins. Because Notre-Dame Cathedral was within walking distance from the hotel, the Gothic structure was at the top of her agenda. It is a place to behold. Following the established practice of church-building — atop pagan sites — during Roman times it was occupied by a temple dedicated to Jupiter. The church, located on an island in the middle of the Seine — where Paris was originally founded in 52 BC — took 182 years to build and was completed in 1345. While Hortensia lit

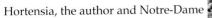

The author with her mother at the Garden
District in New Orleans

Hortensia, the author and Notre-Dame

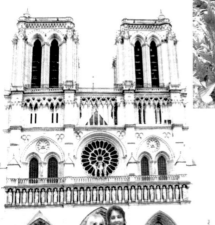

Degas house in Francophile
New Orleans, US

South side (river side) of the Cathedral of Notre-Dame

Notre-Dame Cathedral. North side rose window

Jacint Rigau-Ros i Serr (self-portrait)

The author at Carnavalet

Louis XIV
(by Jacint Rigau-Ros i Serra)

The author at Café Serpente, Chartres

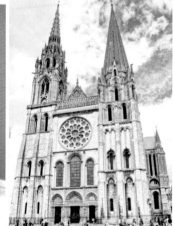

18

Chartres cathedral (1252), SW entrance

half-dozen votive candles around the Cathedral, I walked the length and breadth of the Basilica in awe with its history and ornamentations. Specifically, the rose windows and flying buttresses—a staple style during the Gothic period—that support the weight of the roof. The building also suffered from the anarchy during the French Revolution. It was ransacked early on and later used as a warehouse. Its huge bells melted and turn into cannon ordnance.

Next on her list was the Louvre Museum, another jewel of a place in the French art arsenal. Reading about it is one thing, being there is an overwhelming experience.

Again, the building was something else before it was turned into a museum. In this case it was a castle to protect Paris when the city was a lot smaller back in the 12th Century.

Eventually, the castle gave way to a palace where French kings lived. By the time of Louis XIV's reign, it became just another government building while the Sun King—a self-given moniker—moved house with 7,000 courtiers to the newly built Palace of Versailles in 1682.

The National Assembly made a museum out of the Louvre in 1793 and the emperor renamed it Musée Napoleon in 1801. You can see the enormous 650 square-feet painting of the emperor's coronation by David there, naturally. Being one of the central landmarks of Paris and the second largest in the world with more than 35,000 pieces in display at any one time out of a collection of 350,000 objects, it was Napoleon III (Napoleon Bonaparte's nephew) and his Spanish wife, the Empress Eugénie de Montijo, who turned it into a modern museum as part of his total rejuvenation of Paris from 1853 to 1870.

And what may we find there?: The Winged Victory, the Venus of Milo, the Mona Lisa, Liberty Leading the People... An art lover's dream, it could take a lifetime to see it all, with works by Leonardo de Vinci, Michelangelo, and Raphael, just to name a few of the greats.

A gourmet treat. Not unlike a perpetual motion machine, Hortensia's level of energy was inexhaustible. Able to go for hours on a cup of coffee, after exiting the Louvre she turned to me and, squeezing my hand, said, "Are you hungry?"

And I thought for a moment, am I ever! "Yeah, a bit", I answered.

We crossed rue de Rivoli and, half a block into a side street, we entered a heavily paneled bistro doling out cooked buttery aromas, making my hunger pangs worse. It was my first try at crepes. Filled with gruyere, lean Savoy ham and baked apples, it obliterated my agony in seconds. Never again did crepes tasted so authentic.

Satiated, we took a taxi to rue du Faubourg St-Honore, got off, and strolled down the way to check the latest "chic" apparel—there was one she couldn't resist and didn't. After spending an eternity on that thoroughfare, we visited Chanel at rue Cambon and continued to Galeries Lafayette. There she splurged some more, impulse buying an array of several bottles of very expensive perfume. I still have a long, white scarf with blue flowers she bought me there.

Going back to the hotel—by now Hortensia with swollen feet—we wanted to relax and save energy for a late dinner. Once in our room, she showered and so did I. Afterward, wearing a very feminine blue robe, I laid down on a gorgeous settee or, as the French called it, *lit de repos*, to take a well-deserved breather and listen to my French tapes.

The night was young. After a few hours, I called Gloria and invited her to dinner. She was delighted. When she asked about how the day went at the Louvre, I

Hall of Mirrors at Versailles

Napoleon coronation (detail)

The author on her first trip to Paris

The Winged Victory of Samothrace

The author leaning on a balustrade

George Sand

Honoré de Balsac

Édouard Manet

Luxembourg Gardens and Palace

Sorbonne University. Chapel of Sainte Ursule

The author at the main altar, Chartres cathedral

told her, "inspirational", and promised I would go back to visit the museum with her.

At about nine, we got together and paid a call to a fabulous restaurant Hortensia knew well. It was the perfect ending for a day filled with art.

The next morning after breakfast, we made plans to go to the Luxembourg Garden. We found it in the 6th arrondissement in the heart of Paris's *Rive Gauche* — left bank of the Seine and close to the Latin Quarter. This neighborhood is home to the church *Saint-Germain-des-Pres*, and the elegant garden. The area is considered the soul of Parisian intellectual and cultural life — for Balzac, George Sand, Manet, and the center of the existentialist movement after World War II. Here the Sorbonne is located and where my cousin Gloria was taking language courses. Known for its student life, lively atmosphere and bistros, it reminded me of Harvard Square back in the States. Because Latin was the academic language used at the university in the Middle Ages, this impressive area of Paris is called the Latin Quarter.

The Luxembourg Garden and Palace were engendered by Queen Marie de Medici from 1612 to 1625. She was the widow of King Henry IV. The building served as a royal residence during her regency for her son Louis XIII. During the Revolution it was turned into a prison.

Short of 57 acres with English and French gardens installations, it is actually a park with tree-lined promenades, tennis courts, flowerbeds and marionette shows. The Palace is where the French Senate meets since 1958.

Because I read American writer Gertrude Stein's apartment was nearby, we decided to walk to her place, but it was not open to the public. There is a plaque at No. 27 rue de Fleurus, which marks the importance of this historical, literary address. Her home was a gathering place for writers and artists who would later become famous.

Among them Ernest Hemingway, Scott Fitzgerald, Henri Matisse, Paul Cézanne, and Pablo Picasso, who around 1905 executed a most horrible portrait of her. Stein never spoke to the cubist wonder again; yet, it is considered one of the important works of his Rose Period.

Besides museums and parks, Hortensia also enjoyed visiting a different church every day — there are close to 200 in Paris alone — and she knew most of them. Near the Luxembourg, there is the Church of Saint-Sulpice in the Latin Quarter. It is only slightly smaller than Notre-Dame, and the second largest church in the city. I went in for a while, but attending yet another service didn't appeal to me. Skipping it, I sneaked away and, taking advantage of my brief freedom while Hortensia prayed, I walked around the area to get used to it and get to know it better.

In the coming days, Hortensia and I went to the Eiffel Tower, but first we enjoyed the Trocadero Gardens located across the Seine. This is where travelers come to take pictures of the tower. Paris is filled with gardens. This park was particularly created for the Universal Exposition of 1937. At about 23 acres with powerful water fountains and magnificent sculptures, it delivers a breathtaking view of the Eiffel.

Although now the Tower is truly magnificent, many Parisians hated it as it was being erected. And many eminent intellectuals, including famous French author, Guy de Maupassant, frowned upon it. He called it "a gigantic, black smokestack" that would ruin the beauty of Paris. Yet, today it welcomes almost seven million visitors a year, making it the most visited monument in the world.

Built by Gustave Eiffel — but designed by others — to commemorate the centenary of the French Revolution, the 1,000-foot structure is made of iron that corrodes constantly under wind and precipitation. Hence, parts of it

Queen Marie de Medici

Gertrude Stain (Picasso, 1905-06)

Scott Fitzgerald

Pablo Picasso

Henri Matisse

Paul Cézanne

Trocadero Gardens

Ernest Hemingway and
first wife, Hadley

Hadley Hemingway

Ernest Hemingway and second wife, Pauline

Gustave Eiffel

Hortensia and the author

Guy de Maupassant

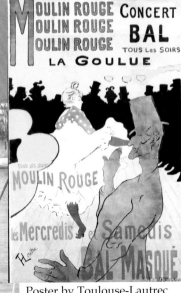

Poster by Toulouse-Lautrec

The author by the Seine in a *bateau mouche*

The enormity of Versailles Palace and a partial view of the famous gardens

Some of the loves of Louis XIV (from left to right):
He wanted to marry Marie Mancini, verboten. Had to wed Maria Theresa of Austria (according to treaty.) Louise de la Valliere became his first mistress of many. Marquise de Maintenon was one of his last mistresses and later spouse.

The author at Les Champs-Elysées

Lovers at the Seine

The famous Moulin Rouge

Parisian dogs

The author at the Louvre

are replaced and painted as needed. So much so that the complete tower has been replaced twice, bit by bit.

Walking away from the Eiffel while taking photographs, we enjoyed the city once more and visited another of the classy restaurants Hortensia knew well. As the sun hid behind western Paris, we headed back to the hotel. Sitting on the balcony and relaxing, we made plans to visit the Versailles Palace the next day.

Although not a Sunday, before touring King Louis XIV's jewel of a dwelling, Hortensia insisted on going to an early mass. Afterward, and way before lunch, we hopped on the train that goes along the Seine, and headed to the Palace located about 15 miles to the west of Paris. Gloria joined us on this trip. She was fun and I was glad she came along.

The Palace. Versailles was built to impress, and the message Louis sent through its architecture was raw, ultimate clout. The muscle employed by the Sun King was quite absolute: He ruled without a customary Chief Minister and declared, "*L'Etat, c'est moi*" [I am the State]. He enjoyed no boundaries and eliminated all rivalries.

Several kings named Louis are connected to the Palace. And of course, France being France, there are also queens and mistresses hitched to the mix; sometimes mistresses trumped the influence of the reigning consort. Broadly speaking, during his monarchy the seat of power was transferred from Paris to Versailles.

Leading through most of the seventy-two years of his run, he begat eighteen offsprings with his two wives (Queen Maria Theresa, who died in 1683, and the Marquise de Maintenon, who he married secretly after the queen died) and many concubines. He died of gangrene at his beloved Estate in 1715.

Neither Napoleon nor Charles X (1824-1830) lived at the Palace; it was costly to run and, after the Revolution, it needed extensive patching up.

Once we arrived there we went straight to the grandiose Hall of Mirrors. It is said the King wanted to show France could produce mirrors just as superior to those produced in Italy. Because, again, he wanted to boast his and France's importance and advancement to the world, he ordered that every accouterment for Versailles must be elaborated by French artisans.

Besides the Hall of Mirrors with over 350 examples—which were valued like diamonds in those days—other outstanding parts of the Palace and grounds we reveled in including the Queen's apartment, the Grand Chapel, the Grand Canal, the gardens and the art collection.

Hortensia had been there before, but there is always something new to discover. We stayed the whole morning, but did not have the chance to visit other buildings around the grounds—they had to wait for later years. We lunched at Versailles and took a late afternoon train back to the city.

Chartres Cathedral. When I thought our days for visiting churches were over, Hortensia, as always, had a new revelation for me. She made plans for us to go to another church!

Short of sixty miles to the west of Paris, it took us a little more than one hour to get there. As we got closer to the town, we took pleasure in the fields of golden sunflowers that were then beginning to bloom.

This is one of the largest Cathedrals in France; it has two asymmetrical towers facing the west entrance and it's an interesting example of gothic design. The church's architecture is magnificent all over. Sitting upon the hill at the center of town, it dominates the view of the countryside. Mythologist Joseph Campbell visited the place many times and said, "...everyone who has spent any time at Chartres has felt something very special about this cathedral."

Once there, we bought a guidebook and ambulated all over the church. I was overwhelmed by its architecture inside and out. The beauty of its stained glass is breathtaking, and the windows which depict biblical stories are just glorious. There are many detailed sculptures embellishing the inside and outside of the Cathedral. We also took the crypt tour to explore the early foundation and history of the Cathedral. I told Hortensia I felt it was the most beautiful church I had seen on this trip. Its composition is magnificent all over. I took some photos and then we climbed the north tower and enjoyed the panoramic view of the small town and its countryside below.

After finishing the church tour we walked around the delightful town until we found the quaint restaurant, *Le Café Serpente*. They serve delicious food, being *rognon de veau* [kidney of veal] one of their specialties, which I ate, but had never tasted. I can say it's an acquired taste, nevertheless. All in all, visiting Chartres Cathedral was a significant adventure.

The Moulin Rouge. After Chartres, the days went rapidly and soon my godmother and I would have to part. Hortensia had promised we could visit the famous cabaret, and we wound up going there on her last night in Paris.

The place that made the scandalous Can-can famous was built in 1889 and commercialized by Joseph Oller and Charles Zidler. This fabulous club is located at the foot of Montmartre hill in the heart of the Pigalle environs in the 18th arrondissement; it is marked by the red windmill on its roof. The Can-can was a seductive dance originally presented by the courtesans who worked from the club site. I was truly excited. It was the first time I tasted champagne. A night I will never forget. As planned, the next day Hortensia left the City of Lights and I was to start art classes. Because the studio Hortensia had arranged for me to stay in was not ready yet, she paid for an extra week at the Sevigne hotel before she left.

Paris and the Seine. The river attracts even those who are indifferent and dull. It would be impossible to think of Paris without the Seine. A delightful waterway with a long history, sometimes serene other times simmering, and many captivating narratives. Paris and the Seine, the Seine and Paris. I don't know who owns who, or if they own each other. No matter, there you'll encounter people fishing, strolling hand-in-hand and hugging along its banks and bridges. The number of famous lovers who frolicked by the Seine is long. From Giacomo Casanova to Porfirio Rubirosa. It is forever the perfect snapshot. In this magnificent place, many have lost themselves in its lyricism. They have left their shyness behind to become part of the magic encircling everything, thus complementing the remarkable spirit of Paris. Those who visit, once they depart, have also left hints of their essence in its winding, old roads, ivy-covered buildings and picturesque quarters. It's a place where everyone strolls or bikes everywhere, even when it's raining. It's the best way to get to know her.

Chestnuts in blossom. I always enjoy walking and, on this trip, meandering around for hours came to me naturally. That is one of the marvelous things about European capitals: locals walk everywhere. Strolling alone now that Hortensia had left, I ventured out of the hotel by turning onto rue de Rivoli. The atmosphere was mesmerizing, and the shades of the clouds made me feel like singing April in Paris. Afraid of being too exuberant, I hummed it instead while rambling all over the quarter; enjoying the moment and taking pics.

A wedding at Pont Alexandre III

Traditional Absinthe

Margaux and the author at Chateau Margaux

Madame Sévigné

The author and Gloria at Pont Alexandre III

Cannalé

Café Noisette

Frederic Chopin

Alfred de Musset

The author across the Eiffel Tower (spring always brings rain)

The author at Picasso museum

The author at Versailles

The author outside the Opera

The author inside the Opera

Gallery Louis XVI at Carnavalet

Former ballroom from the Hôtel de Wendel by José M. Sert (1925)

Paris Opera

All around me in the Marais there were signs of real Parisian life. Children walking to school, recent mothers taking their infants for a stroll, and the young and the old walking their dogs. Those precious canines are cherished by the French almost as much as their children. They are proud of their pooches, which they see as part of the family and, most of the time, are well groomed. It seems everyone in the city has a dog, and they own many different breeds — expecting poodles, that day I didn't see one.

Strolling leisurely from the Marais toward Champs-Elysees — *la plus belle avenue du monde* — the rays from the sun felt comfy. Strolling northwest on rue de Rivoli towards the Place de la Concorde, dogs kept increasing in numbers. It was such a curious sight that they became the subjects for some snapshots, together with their owners. It is one of those rare occasions when Parisians will smile; even showing some dentition. It was nice. Broad smiles are not part of the culture of these city dwellers. Not even waiters will crack a grin — no small wonder the tip is always included in the bill.

Alert walking provides the benefit of facing a variety of interesting subjects to capture, and cats are not an exception. Unlike dogs, which can be annoyingly friendly, a cat's apathy and aplomb can be a source of prejudice. Yet, I believe their disdain can make them as beautiful as dogs are chummy. But there weren't many cats — except in the fish market — running around or sitting at window sills. Such a pity. Cats are animals with so much aloofness that they would be perfect in Paris. I might be wrong, but the French lack a cat culture. At least in Paris, anyway.

About two miles into my walk, always heading west, I suddenly came upon a beautiful bride and her photographer at Pont Alexandre III — a most dazzling bridge. The bride and groom, a stunning Asian-French couple, were having the time of their lives. Asking them if they were models, they shook their heads. Like any other bride and groom in the world, emotions were flying high, including my own.

I crossed the bridge from side to side looking for that unique site or subject to photograph. Buildings, churches, fountains, monuments, babies, dogs, flowers, young people, refined older gentlemen, and of course ladies coiffured and dressed in dark colors ensembles.

Continuing to saunter and taking lots of pictures of the Seine and its bridges, there at my feet was the famous waterway immortalized by painters and poets bringing romantic images of bygone days, and present pleasurable and loving experiences.

J'adore manger. By one o'clock I was ready for lunch. Walking around was a trip all by itself, but the body needs nourishment, liquids, rest and perhaps some sweets, preferably chocolate. A *cafe au lait* and a croissant at a charming tea house two hours into my walk had done the trick, but the long trek made me hungry. Staying away from famous bistros frequented by known American writers—Henry Miller, Hemingway, Fitzgerald and Zelda—and recommended by my friend, the painter Enrique Riverón, I paused in front of a brasserie at rue de Ponthieu—also mentioned by a guest at the hotel—and went inside. Casing the place, it seemed most of the patrons were local and the dining room wasn't crowded. By the window, my preferred spot was waiting. While settling at my table, next to me an older gentleman glanced in my direction as he sat holding hands with a petite young woman. Without missing a beat, he whispered in her ear and she seemed to enjoy his mumbling, apparently agreeing with the old fellow. I wondered if they were married—something doubtful. Perhaps *une maîtresse.*

After a short wait, the waitress showed up with pen and paper. A matron with square hips and a bit overweight, she didn't fit the Parisian anyone could imagine. A pleasant lady with a slightly unfamiliar accent, she asked if she could be of service. Still looking at the menu and trying to practice my French, curious, I asked her: *"Vous venez de Paris?"* Saying no and smiling, she told me her place of birth was Budapest and that her family lived close to the Danube. Such a romantic setting. Rivers are my thing. When she finally took my order I decided to start with an absinthe-flavored innocent drink; when it came, it needed a dash of sugar to make it better. In Oscar Wilde's appraisal of the real, unadulterated drink he said, "After the first glass, you see things as you wish they were, after the second one you see things as they are not."

With my glass close to empty, the good woman was ready with my lunch: *coq au vin* served with mushrooms and asparagus spears, a perfect spring vegetable. To drink, just sparkling water. Holding down the weight is hard to do when meals are delicious. So I skipped formal dessert and opted instead to pop into my mouth a small, dark chocolate bon-bon with an almond in the middle, kept in my purse away from the probing eyes of the staff in restaurants. I stayed for a while to draft a to-do list — they never rush you in Parisian restaurants.

A short while later, a new waiter approached the table — apparently, the Hungarian lady had finished her shift — to see if he could be of service. A man in his early forties and very congenial, Armand, came from the Languedoc-Roussillon region and spoke pretty good English. He was an "exile" from a southern province, the refined man explained. His family had been Occitans for generations and Armand missed his culture and land, where the climate is benign and its people were warmer; nevertheless, jobs were not as easy to come by as in Paris. We talked about art and history. To my surprise, the gentleman was pleasing and open in his conversation, something you hardly find in Paris.

Locals in the big cities tend to be introverted, specifically waiters, who are usually not too affable. Although lunch wasn't huge, sleepiness caught me off-guard; therefore, Armand brought me a *café noisette* [espresso with a thimbleful of milk]. The French usually don't drink it after dinner, but I enjoy it.

Lingering a little longer to make notes and consult the map, I wanted to make sure not to lose time wandering in circles; there were lots of *rues* to cover. Because, like true lovemaking, Paris is made of unique moments, the meal hit the spot and was fairly priced. Paying the waiter, who was still talking, he walked me to the door. The place was almost empty. My guess was that everybody had gone back to work.

A chance encounter. Leaving the small eatery, I looked up to check the weather and take the fresh air when, in a sudden move, my camera flew from my hands—luckily it was wrapped around my neck—as a nice-looking man bumped into me. He apologized immediately while holding my right elbow to stop me from falling—I wasn't—and the waiter took notice and stepped away from the threshold of the entrance. The server, already on the sidewalk, greeted the stranger and shook his hand, asking him how a certain venture was coming along. *"Ça va bien"*, he answered, smiling in my direction still yo-yoing the waiter's hand. Looking into my eyes and introducing himself in French, he realized I spoke English and, glancing at my camera, asked to take a peek at it. He was carrying one himself which looked beaten to a pulp. Returning it, the man said, "nice, are you a tourist?" Explaining my situation as a student and amateur photographer visiting the city on a personal project and for art classes, excitedly he exclaimed: "So am I. I'm here to tell a story in pictures, except that I've been working at it for the last eight years".

"Hold it", I said, "Let's hope it doesn't take me that long", rolling my eyes in disbelief.

"You can always come back and we can exchange ideas", he said flirtatiously. To cool things off I changed the subject.

Smiling I said, "By the way, my friends call me Nildi", while extending my hand.

He asked Armand for *deux café* and invited me to sit at a table outside. I did, but waved off the coffee.

His name was Scott. Tall, with light skin, medium-brown hair, and a square Irish jaw, this guy reminded me of the boys I went to school with. He had a pleasant smile. "That's a very masculine name. Never met anyone named Scott", I told him. He explained his grandmother had named him after Scott Fitzgerald, one of her favorite writers. This Scott, who was also an American, had a friendly demeanor and explained he had lived for several years in Paris with his parents when he was a kid. In his teens he had gone back to the States to continue his schooling, then, upon graduation from college, decided to move back to Paris for a short period. Those were the plans; however, the longer he stayed, the bigger his interest grew.

"So you see, my project kept growing in my head, and so, I'm still here", he said laughing. I told him it would be nice to stay longer, but that my time was limited, assuring him—sounding positive—the time available was enough to complete my undertaking. Filled with optimism, I gave him a big, wide smile. "Well, you never know", he said. "The idea might keep developing and then it owns you." He declared convincingly.

Getting up, I said, "really should be going. Must discover a lot more before it gets dark. And I'm meeting my cousin, who is here with me."

"Wait, wait, have you seen the city at night?", he asked.

"With my godmother", I explained. She just left for Spain."

"Well, have you seen it from the river at dusk? You'll find dawn and dusk have hues perfect for photography", he continued. "If you let me, I'll be your guide," Scott said enthusiastically. Reassessing the moment and feeling he was a nice guy, although my parents would have been worried, the idea sounded appealing.

"Yes, why not," I answered.

"And if you want, we could talk about all your plans and compare notes. Where are you staying?", he said.

"In the Marais. A quaint, little place off rue Rivoli, near Saint-Paul station", I offered. Sensing there was no harm in sharing information for, after all, they knew him at the restaurant. The thought of having a near-native who spoke English showing me around and getting to know the city was too tempting.

"I will pick you up early in the evening", he assured me.

"Fine, what about seven? You will be on time, right?", I said knowing he would, waving goodbye and laughing while walking away.

From the restaurant's door, he shouted "Do you like jazz? Oh!, wait a minute, which hotel?".

"Yes, jazz is fine. Madame de Sevigne in rue Malher!" Starting towards him to avoid shouting.

"Well", he said, "there are some fun clubs in Montmartre where you can still enjoy it. If you allow me, I'd love to invite you and your cousin. By the way, did you know Scott Fitzgerald coined the phrase the Jazz Age?"

"Yes, read some of his stories. The Great Gatsby was excellent, it will be fun to listen to jazz in Paris like in

Victor Hugo and his famous desk

Alexandre Dumas

Balzac's mother

Balzac's house

Bertrade de Montfort

The author at Fontainebleau's chapel

The author at Fontainebleau

Christina, Queen of Sweden

Marriage of Louis XV

Luncheon on the Grass by Monet

Victor Hugo's Place des Vosges

Luncheon on the Grass by Manet

Rock formations at Barbizon   49

From L to R: Daniel, the author and Scott.

Jean Cocteau

Colette

Marla and the author at Barbizon

the old days", I said eagerly. Turning away waving and parting again.

Looking straight into the distance of the narrow street, cheerful and charmed, thinking it was going to be an even more pleasant trip than envisioned, I then pictured what my immalleable godmother—a woman of the world—would have said about this honest encounter. Smirking and shaking my head, I kept on walking.

A drizzle began to fall off and on while walking the quarters. Reflecting for a moment, the darkening skies made me feel isolated. Still, I took a few more pictures until a restlessness invaded. With a long walk ahead of me and figuring it was time to head back to the hotel, I put away the camera and continued to backtrack according to the map. Crossing to rue Rivoli, the neighborhood began to look familiar. Near Rivoli and Ferdinand Duval, I dropped the film at the photo shop as the sun made its appearance again—that's springtime in Paris. After passing by a *charcuterie* and saying to myself, there is dinner, I crossed the street and went into the cute deli. Because my lunch had left me satisfied, supper was going to be simple and easy; besides, Scott was treating later on.

From the delicatessen, walking out with a ham sandwich with tomato and goat cheese on a perfectly crispy bread sprinkled with olive oil, which is a passion with me, my mouth watered. It was the type of bread only the French can make. To wash it down, a small bottle of soft cider did the trick.

Finally I was back at the hotel, and instead of watching television, rested, took a shower, and ate my delicious sandwich while listening to Edith Piaf's[1] tapes. Coincidentally with the last bite, the photos had to be ready. I slowly got dressed and went back to rue Rivoli.

Taking my time eye-scanning the images and realizing I liked them all, leisurely, the walk back to the hotel turned into entertainment as a street performer caught my eye playing a very romantic sonata for viola.

Once in my room, I laid down my evening clothes and relaxed while now listening to my French tapes. Promising myself to add a few more expressions to my vocabulary each day, each word coming out hopefully sounded better. I also called Gloria to let her know about Scott, just to be on the safe side. She thought the whole situation was delightful and agreed not to mention it to my parents. Asking her to come along, she claimed her friend had invited her to a club and we could meet the next day. That was fine, I knew Gloria loved dancing and probably had already met with her friend's brother, for she had talked about him endlessly and was smitten by the guy, notwithstanding her boyfriend in Barcelona.

As promised, Scott was calling from the lobby a few minutes after seven. I found him all shaved and perfumed; he held both of my hands and gave me the usual compliments. Reacting pleasantly surprised, it seemed that, when it came to timekeeping, he was not like the French or the Spaniards.

While crossing the street, Scott mentioned about taking a trip in the *bateau mouche*—a fly-boat. Puzzled, I asked: "At night, a flying boat?"

"No, no", he chuckled. "It's a riverboat. They happen to call fly-boat to riverboats. It is a cruise along the Seine showcasing outstanding views of the city. It's a great way to explore Paris. They are offered during the day and night. They start right at the foot of the Eiffel Tower and go all the way past *Île de la Cite* and back. It takes about one hour. I'm sorry, but if that is too lovey-dovey for you, we could take it during the day."

"Well", I said laughing. "I'm cool to the idea. It sounds fantastic." Thinking to myself, well, he is amusing and sociable, feeling safe in his presence.

"Look", he said, "on the trip, you'll be able to see the old buildings and monuments all lit up. They will share the history of the city and point out sites such as the Grand and Petit Palaces, the National Assembly, the Musée d'Orsay, the Ile de la Cite and many others."

We walked quietly for about a minute and it felt awkward. Breaking the silence I said: "Oh, yes, I remember now. Audrey Hepburn and Cary Grant did it in Charade. Did you see the flick?"

"Yes, many years ago", he answered, "I like those types of films". Near the Saint-Paul metro station, he hailed a cab and we headed to the Eiffel Tower.

Drifting downstream. We boarded the boat. There was a soft, cool, but comfortable breeze by the dock, so we decided to sit outside. The view was amazing. Because my camera was back at the hotel, I had the time to take in the scenery without a lens blocking my view; luckily, Scott had brought his and took a photo of me standing by the rail. Slowly we motored against the Seine current up to and beyond the *Île Saint-Louis* and back. This gave me time to talk about my project and for him to share his. Although we were both using a camera, the aim of how to present Paris to the world could not have been more different. I held a romantic view and his was more realistic, perhaps mordant. Maybe that was why I was so curious about him.

After our river ride ended, we walked around for a while. At any hour of the day, the city is always dazzling and enigmatic at the same time, like a mature woman who forever knows how to present herself. Scott also suggested that during the day I should take the *batobus*. It's a shuttle service that allows you to board at any of eight stops, whenever you please. Planning to walk all through the city, and because rivers are a passion with me, eventually I bought a pass and used it for transportation during the day.

Scott had mentioned his friend Mimi was coming with us. We made the acquaintance and then continued to the jazz club. The three of us got there and, as we sat in a barely lit corner, two other girls who knew Scott came over to say hello and joined us for a while. The group listened to jazz, consumed some vittles, and then the girls and Mimi left with their boyfriends, as Scott invited me to walk around the area. But my feet were killing me. Concerned, he invited me to an all-night tea house for a cup and I gladly accepted. The night had turned cold. Once we got there, a tea called *Mont Rouge* animated my fancy. The spicy, fragrant brew and a petite brioche roll fixed me up. He had a cup of wine. Like in Spain, in France a special occasion is not needed to savor a glass; anytime is appropriate. Once silly, the conversation turned enlightening. We compared notes once more. Sharing that, aside from his photographic project, he also wrote articles for travel magazines all around the globe and in different languages. Because of this, he claimed his life was always "go, go, go", traveling mostly in Europe and the Arab countries. "I'm fluent in Arabic", he added.

It was one in the morning when we finally got back to the Marais, my surroundings and sweet-home for the whole spring. It had been a long, intense day and I yearned for more. Glad that my classmates were not with me now, in a way, I wouldn't have liked to share my new found friend.

The front desk clerk said Gloria had called. Tired, and ready for bed, I said good night and Scott went on his way warbling a tune, but not before he asked to come by later that morning. "Of course", I said, "but not too early. It has been a very busy day for me, Scott, and I need to rest."

"Fine, then I'll call to make sure you're up to it." Before he left, he mentioned once more how enchanted he was about my project, and how he wanted to be my guide for the rest of my stay to see how it developed. I accepted gladly. After all, what harm could come from it?

By late morning I enjoyed room service and was dressed, ready and excited with my new plan. Deciding to wear beige pants with a light pink blouse, and, for my feet, a pair of comfortable hot pink espadrilles bought at a flea market, I finally phoned Gloria to make new plans. We talked about Scott and the jazz club. Captivated and fascinated with my escapades and new friend, she and I agreed to meet later in the day.

Scott arrived promptly and called from the lobby. On the phone he said he'd come up with a "phenomenal" idea—he used the word a lot. Because the morning was still windy and nippy, I toted along a lightweight, beige jacket my aunt Ofelia gifted me from her visit to Madrid. For an accent, a multi-colored hot pink and beige scarf wrapped around my neck complemented the outfit, to keep me warm. I had, without a doubt, a color-coordinated ensemble that would clash with the quintessential Parisien who usually wears dark colors, especially in brisk weather. Because Paris has been for ages the capital of haute couture, their habit of wearing subdued colors most of the time is a conundrum. It seems a contradiction exists for a city to be called *"la Ville Lumiere"* but its women refuse to be color-matched. To me—and science— light is color and color is light. Except for kids, I guess, it is easier to just wear drabness, even in summer—at least that was my experience.

Grabbing my camera and a few other things, we met in the lobby. He seemed excited, and said he wanted to introduce me to a polite French lady. "Her name is Margaux, she has a guest room and sometimes rents it to female students", he explained. "She's a widow who was married to an American executive." Scott clarified he met Margaux through her husband at a party in the American Embassy. Presently she was alone, but he was sure she would be glad to put me up. Because the couple never had children, my presence would be beneficial. He added, "you'll practice your French."

"Well", I reacted with a chuckle, "let's hope she doesn't want to practice her English."

"No, no", Scott emphasized, "she speaks English well and will be patient with you. Margaux is an angel. She's not the kind of Parisian lady who might get flustered with every word you garble."

Before leaving, I called Gloria once more to let her know about the new plan.

A happening day. Margaux's pad was in the 4th arrondissement, right in Île St-Louis, a walking distance from Notre-Dame. Scott mentioned that from her window on the fourth floor, there was an impressive view of the old cathedral towers. I thought about it for a few minutes and then agreed to meet her. He had already spoken to her about me that morning and called her to let her know we would be dropping by.

Deciding to walk to her place, at Rivoli we took a right and then a left at Fourcy. Fourcy becomes d'Hyeres and takes you straight to Pont Marie crossing. We walked around the island till we could see the famous cathedral. Shooting several pics while taking advantage it was early and not too many people were around, I said, "let's come back later, cross the bridge to Notre-Dame and climb to the top of the tower."

Scott responded with "phenomenal", again. Almost there, Scott mentioned Margaux's family was from the southern region of Bordeaux and for generations were engaged in the production of wine. "Expect a lot of wine around her home", Scott advised me. "Not everyone in Paris has such a stash".

"Spain is the same. Wine on the table and off is a must. They serve it at every meal", I said.

Margaux was waiting for us. Slow-walking around Quai d'Orléans for about twenty minutes got us there.

When she opened the door, a lovely lady appeared. A table set with refreshments in a nearby room was waiting for us. From a distance you could smell the delicious buttery aroma — to die for — of baked *madeleines*; I also saw a few other delicacies with chocolate and fruit. The room was infused with the fragrance of fresh-brewed coffee and I got giddy. Because in the morning a strong brew is my pleasure and the walk to her place was lengthy, I was in the mood for another cup. Getting used to sipping coffee in my teen years, to my glee, I found French espresso similar to the one my mother made.

Scott was right. She was polite, approachable and very friendly. At medium height, her hair was white, softly waved and short, but not too short. Very well dressed, she reminded me of actress Catherine Deneuve, except she was not aloof suchlike the French cinematic star in *Belle de jour*.

Margaux's smile was open and pleasant. Suddenly, all my doubts about the French character were erased, at least in her case.

"Meet Nildi", Scott said. Margaux said *bonjour* and kissed me on both cheeks. After exchanging pleasantries, we sat and talked for a while enjoying the delicious snacks. She wanted to know what had brought me to Paris. I explained the plan of taking art classes and also the photography project with the idea of a student exhibit on my return to the States.

"Well, my interests are a mixed bag", I said. "Besides poetry, photography is one of those endeavors that excite me." I continued. "The experience of traveling and taking photographs of all things appealing allows me to write better. I feel there is a cordial relationship between poetry and photography."

"Well, it all sounds very exciting", she said. "It's a wonderful way to stay involved in life." Scott nodded. I noticed he was writing in a notebook and then asked if he could use the phone.

"Margaux, there are many people who want to come to this incredible city all their lives and probably would never be able to do so", I asserted. "In the thirties, someone like Hemingway could live here for a fraction of the cost of living in New York or Boston."

"Not now", she interrupted. "Paris is as expensive as New York. Especially for students; they've been priced out."

"I know. But those are my dreams. I imagine myself moving amid my exhibit full of visitors and answering questions about my experience."

"Yes, you're right. I see your point", she said smiling.

"That's one of the many things I want to do after college. To someday share my work." I said animatedly. She seemed pleased with my ideas. Then Margaux told me that if I wanted to stay with her, she would welcome me with open arms. Her soft-sounding accent was impeccable and not guttural, like the French sometimes resonate. There wasn't anything to think about. Accepting the invite right away and asking her if it was possible to practice my dreadful French with her, I ventured, "I've been taking lessons for a while but it's hard to be fluent without immersion. I want to get the most out of this trip."

"You're correct", she said.

The opportunity of practicing with a native was important. My wish was to at least be able to carry a short conversation with a few French acquaintances back in the States. I wanted to impress them. The chat took place while we all enjoyed the repast.

"Do you speak any other language?", she asked.

"Yes. My mother tongue is Spanish, and of course in the States English in school. I've always enjoyed communicating with other cultures. Next year I'll try my hand at various Romance languages. But French has proven more difficult than what I thought", I said.

"True, French is not an easy language. There are a lot of rules and accents", she said.

"Well, talking to one of my teachers, an American raised in France, I said that losing my Spanish accent while speaking French would be challenging. But the funny thing was what she answered. She told me, 'it's fine, who cares, I never lost my Louisiana accent, either'".

"Incidentally, my husband's family is from Texas", Margaux said, "and he was raised in New York. It was hard for me to understand them when we visited Dallas. But they liked me and all of us spoke slower, and they didn't mind my accent, either", she shared smiling.

"Well, most people are tolerant", I answered. I thought about the mixture of cultures and how beneficial they can be. She's from my tribe, I reasoned. "Anyway, I would appreciate it if I could practice French with you." She laughed and agreed to help me.

"You show *joie de vivre*, my dear, which is a very French trait. You're ahead already. I will help you if you agree to speak Spanish to me once in a while." She said.

"It's a deal", I jumped at the suggestion. Margaux explained she had also taken Spanish lessons when she was younger and had meant to start again. With her husband she traveled all over the world, but Spain had always been a favorite place to visit.

"I even made plans to stay for a while in Seville when the April Fair is on, go to El Prado in Madrid, learn to dance Flamenco, but my life got complicated now that my husband is gone. Perhaps next year I'll go. In any case, his affairs are settled", using these last words as her eyes lit up.

"Perhaps we could go together", I suggested.

"Oh, yes, and we can ride carriages drawn by gorgeous horses and dress like a *Sevillana*", she responded.

While Scott was on the phone, we drank coffee and I enjoyed looking at the photographs she had taken with her many *españoles* friends. Her Spanish hostess in Seville, she explained, was in her fifties, still looked attractive and, according to what Margaux described, very up-to-date and did not act like the typical woman of her age. The kind of lady who knew what she wanted out of life. I found Margaux's experiences and contacts intriguing and felt she was probably the same way. I noticed, "Well, you know, Thatcher Ulrich did write 'Well-behaved women seldom make history'".

"So true," she said smiling.

What an interesting circle of friends my new landlady had, I thought. She was certainly well-connected.

Margaux continued. "I want to visit my friend in Seville. Maybe she can introduce me to a nice, unattached gentleman."

"Good for you", I rejoined. "Nowadays there are no age barriers for women to have fun." She seemed pleased with my assertion.

Margaux then got up and said, "Come with me, I want to show you your bedroom." We walked down a spacious hall, stopping at a white and gold-colored door and she revealed the room that would become my new retreat in Paris. It was spacious, painted in light blue, with a single bed, a desk, drawer chess and, on top of it, a gold-leafed mirror. There was also adequate closet space, an art nouveau table with drawers and a table lamp in the same style. Besides, the room had a large window from where one could see a charming rose garden; the setting was perfect and my chance rendezvous with Scott was paying

60

dividends. Unintentional, personal brushes don't have to end this well.

After Scott finished on the phone, he caught our attention and said, "sorry I've got to go to turn in an article right now." And he was out the door.

Turning to me, Margaux said, "when he comes back tonight, I'll open a bottle of Chateau Margaux to celebrate this lovely encounter. A perfect time to tell you the history of the wine."

Before she began to share another story, I glanced at my watch and said, "Oh my, we're having such a marvelous time that I forgot my list of things to do. Sorry, but I should get going."

"Yes, of course you must. Then I'll be expecting you", she said.

Finally, when her telephone rang, it was my chance to clear out. As she lifted the receiver, in a lower voice I said, "à plus tard", and walked out.

Excited, from the first public telephone I found I called Gloria and left her a message: "J'ai trouvé un endroit", [I found a place.]

With a busy day ahead of me, I probed the museums and determined it was best to start by visiting the Musée Carnavalet[2] at 23 rue de Sévigné, dedicated to the history of Paris. The idea was to get a feeling of Paris through its history, before taking more photographs.

The Carnavalet Museum was not far from Margaux's place. It's the first venue anyone visiting Paris should discover. While walking, I kept thinking about my project. Paris, with its glorious surroundings and nearby towns, was a perfect subject for what I had in mind. It was stimulating to know that by the end of my journey it was going to be a difficult task to cull the best images. My art teacher kept reminding me space at the new school gallery was small. "You'll only be able to show four photographs, at most", ran through my mind. It would be arduous indeed to pick out the ones I preferred. At the moment all I had was hope. Hope to someday having a solo exhibition and even sell a couple of prints. Walking and day-dreaming were two of my favorite activities.

In due time the facade of Carnavalet was in front of me. The capital's most authentic museum, it is also the most interesting. A blend of five centuries of French architecture and originally a residence, the building was constructed in 1548 and is one of the oldest in the city. But the history of this former townhouse as a museum is intriguing.

In 1866, at the encouragement of Baron Georges-Eugène Haussmann,[3] who was demolishing some of the oldest parts of Paris, the city council bought the building to house the new institution. The renovation of Paris was a vast public works program commissioned by Emperor Napoléon III[4] and directed by Haussmann himself between 1853 and 1870. His charge was to make Paris a livable place, which was a reasonable goal considering how dirty and crime-ridden Paris was, but also to show the world how successful and wealthy France had become.

Related to the first Napoleon by way of Louis, his brother, the Third wanted Paris to be the center of world culture and politics—and he was indeed successful at that. Married to the ebullient Eugénie de Montijo [1853] and encouraged by her, the works included the demolition of crowded and unhealthy medieval neighborhoods, the laying out of wide avenues, parks and squares, and the construction of a new sewer system, fountains and aqueducts. It was then that the idea of a place devoted to the history of Paris became a reality when a large portion of the timeworn heart of Paris was being knocked down. In visiting the exhibitions, we see pieces from prehistoric days to the present. There is a river canoe dating back to 4,600 BC, old documents and furniture. Enjoying the design of interiors, I was delighted to find there complete

62

layouts salvaged from the ravaged buildings; they show the development of how wealthy Parisians lived from the 17th to the 20th Centuries—all exceptionally elaborated and beautiful.

Notwithstanding being a historical museum, it is also a gorgeous gallery where one can enjoy not only *objets d'art* but also posters and drawings. In an accurate setting, I walked through one hundred rooms. For those who like Art Deco, there is the elegant ballroom taken from the hôtel de Wendel and painted in 1925 by Catalan muralist José María Sert.[5] The artist was the son of an affluent family in the textile industry and a friend of Salvador Dalí.

I was enriched by examining the private lives of famous Parisians. For example, inspecting the Marquise de Sévigné's charming Chinese lacquered writing desk, one can imagine the marquise writing her famous letters—a practice I also enjoy. It was exciting to delve into Marcel Proust's bedroom, his brass bed and his little table covered with pens, ink and notebooks. Perhaps it was there where he wrote *Remembrance of Things Past,* and also his many letters. Fancy him fragile, sitting down and looking into space while invoking the experiences of his youth.

From the beginning, the works of art found at the museum delighted me: The historical scenes of the city and portraits of well-known individuals from all walks of life; the architectural designs; interior decorations; wallpapers; bric-a-brac porcelains. While there among the paintings, I polished up on the French Revolution,[6] one of my favorite periods in political history, and the Paris Commune.[7] They conjure images of George Sand, the cutting-edge author and activist who used a man's name to get published, walking the streets of Paris with her children in tow after leaving her husband to continue her love affair with Alfred de Musset; and later with Frederick Chopin, among others.

The museum began with only one building, but it kept expanding and, since 1989, it has occupied the adjoining building. It also houses the Gallo-Roman collection. Nowadays we can still enjoy the fabulous French gardens. In love with colors and greenery, I sauntered among hundreds of plants and was in awe with the arc de Nazareth, which is a magnificent Renaissance structure taken from the *Île de la Cité*.

Eugenia de Montijo. Studying the urban renewal that yielded "modern Paris", which began in 1853, I discovered Spaniard Eugenia de Montijo (1826-1920) was actually the driving force behind many of the projects defining such a colossal enterprise. As empress consort of France, she helped her husband beautify the city and especially promoted the organization of what is now called The Louvre Museum in Paris. Eugenia or Eugénie, had an abundant education, spoke three languages, and understood art and fashion quite well. With her novel ideas she encouraged esthetics above all.

Born in Granada, during her girlhood in Spain she was known as Doña María Eugenia Ignacia Agustina de Palafox y Kirkpatrick, later Countess of Montijo. As a young woman, she left for Paris where she attended the Convent of the Sacré Coeur. Later, she moved to Bristol (UK) to attend a boarding school to learn English. A curious adventurer, she had the chance to travel and discover different cultures; consequently, preparing her for what life could present in the future. She was what we now call an "independent mind." She knew she was attractive with a good figure, but she also wished to be known as bright and astute. That is something Napoleon III realized early on and why, although there were many young women with more important titles than her, he decided to

Napoléon III with Eugenie and son

The Empress in her hayday

Statue of the Empress

Louis-Napoléon,
Prince Imperial

Louvre Museum Apollon gallery

Napoléon III's room

Fourth from the left, the Empress and her ladies in waiting

marry Eugénie in 1853. She represented the Emperor in many venues, including the opening of the Suez Canal in 1869. Eugénie was the guest of honor at the festival and, during her visit, a main street in Port Said was named after her. Although the name has been changed, people still refer to it as "Eugénie Street". In meeting Napoleon III at a party, he was smitten by her and asked: "How do I get to your heart?" and she immediately answered: "Through the chapel, sir." A young woman with a strong personality that knew her worth, she was not about to become his mistress. In a speech on 22 January 1853, Napoleon III, after becoming emperor, formally announced his engagement, saying, "I have preferred a woman whom I love and respect to a woman unknown to me, with whom an alliance would have had advantages mixed with sacrifices."

Their only son, Louis-Napoléon, Prince Imperial, was born in March 1856 at the Tuileries Palace in Paris, and he was baptized on 14 June 1856 at Notre Dame Cathedral.

Eugénie managed to play a feminist role when being a feminist was politically incorrect. In her own time, she was touting for female education and advocated the recognition of women's achievements in literature, arts, and education. This was the time when women writers had to use a pseudonym to get published, like Amantine-Lucile-Aurore Dudevant, who adopted the name George Sand for her novels and the empress lobbied to get her inducted into the French Academy and failed. Empress Eugénie was very clever and had become a good friend to Queen Victoria. She managed to form an excellent political relationship between England and France. When the emperor was deposed after France's defeat at the Battle of Sedan in May 1871, the empress and her husband took permanent refuge in England and settled at Camden Place in Chislehurst, Kent. Napoleon III died on January

9, 1873. On his father's death, young Louis-Napoleon was proclaimed by the Bonapartist faction as Napoleon IV. A few years after his father's death, the Prince Impérial also died on 1 June 1879. In England, he had trained as a soldier and, serving with British forces, he was killed during the Zulu War in South Africa. His early death caused an international debate as he was the last serious dynastic hope for the restoration of the House of Bonaparte to the throne of France. Eugénie lived a long life in exile, dying at the age of 94 in July 1920, while visiting the Liria Palace in Madrid—her grandnephew, Jacobo, XVII Duke of Alba, owned Liria. He was the father to the much admired Cayetana, XVIII Duchess of Alba, who died at the Palacio de las Dueñas (Seville) on 20 November 2014, at the age of 88. She was succeeded by her son Carlos Fitz-James Stuart, 19th Duke of Alba, who now resides in Liria. According to her wishes, Eugenia, the former empress, was buried, along with her husband and her only son, at St Michael's Abbey, Farnborough (UK).

Marquise de Sevigne.[8] One of the most interesting tenants of the Carnavalet, before it became a museum, was the Parisien, marquise de Sévigné (1626-1696). The mansion was the residence of the Marquise from 1677 until she died while visiting her daughter, Françoise-Marguerite de Sévigné, comtesse de Grignan, in Provence. De Sevigne's story is fascinating. Her maiden name was Marie Rabutin-Chantal. She also had a son named Charles. I came to know of her after staying at the eponym of the hotel. It was then I began to look for information about her life and learned she became contemporarily famous in letter-writing. Because it piqued my curiosity and I love the epistolary craft, I had to find out more about this fascinating woman. She belonged to an ancient, aristocratic Burgundian family and had married young to a womanizing Breton in 1644. Unfortunately and eventually, her husband was fatally wounded in a duel over a woman, and he died two days later. Because in those days it was customary among the upper classes to marry their daughters to the right and well-connected man, which usually meant a groom much older than the bride, I asked myself if she suffered the loss or was relieved that he was gone.

At twenty-five and still beautiful, she went back to Paris society and frequented literary salons, especially one sponsored by Nicolas Fouquet, superintendent of finances to King Louis XIV. Although the Marquise had many offers, she never remarried and dedicated herself to her children. In 1676 she became seriously ill and went to Vichy to find a cure with the thermal waters there, where she finally recovered. The letters to her friends describing life at this 17th Century spa are among her best. In those letters, and the ones she sent to family members, she gives a magnificent insight into the Paris of her day, and other parts of France she knew well.

Marie's correspondence became popular, so much so that the missives were copied and shared with others to keep people entertained. Her letters are fascinating, sometimes amusing, other times serious, and all are an important testament of the time. Once she knew that even strangers were reading them, she applied herself with more enthusiasm, thus sharing information about court customs, dresses, and hat styles of the day. She covered everything: Vacations, political gossip, trials and executions, including obituaries of other writers and friends. The daughter, Françoise Marguerite, developed into a vain and cold person who couldn't find a suitor. She was finally able to marry at twenty-three—late for the 17th Century when many women died early. According to her cousin, Roger de Bussy-Rabutin,[9] she made as many enemies as her mother made friends. The husband, a nobleman from Provence not famous for his looks, was 36 years old and twice a widower. They left Paris to live at his estate after he was named lieutenant-general of the Provence region by Louis XIV. When Françoise left, her mother became miserable. It was then when her correspondence to her daughter, who she doted, began. The missives filled ten volumes in the latest edition. In almost thirty years, de Sevigne sent over 1,000 letters to her daughter, usually composing twenty pages a day. Most of them written while living at Carnavalet. They are a good example of why it's important to leave a legacy through writings, paintings or photography, and why the museum is still connected to the Marquise.

After visiting the Musée Carnavalet and learning a lot more about the exciting French history, I called Gloria again. We met at her friend's apartment and walked together to Pont Alexandre III. There we sat for a while engrossing in everyday Parisian life and talking about my new place. The afternoon weather kept its resplendence as people walked their dogs and the young had fun. We stayed by the Seine savoring the romantic view, while my camera kept on clicking snapshots till the sun began to set over the Eiffel Tower.

Bidding *adieu* to Gloria, I went back to Margaux's to practice my French and to also let her chat in Spanish, as promised. Then, early that evening, I went back to the hotel, retrieved my suitcase and relocated with Margaux. We sure made a fabulous team and continued to have a ball throughout my stay at her tony residence. It also became the start of a lasting friendship.

One afternoon after my art class, to my surprise, Scott was at Margaux's enjoying a bottle of slightly sparkling wine. I hadn't seen him for a few days. We all sat talking while biting on pieces of sliced, cured meats. I mentioned my accomplishments of the last few days while he relished the wine with "mmm!" and "ah!"

At some point, Margaux said, "It's one of my favorite wines, Scott, and I'm glad you like it. It was named in my honor."

"Wow, lovely." I exclaimed. "And these Belgian biscuits are terrific. By the way, Scott mentioned your family has been in wine production for generations." Putting his glass down, Scott then asked to use the phone and Margaux assented.

"That's true," she confirmed. "My family's name was Lestonnac several centuries back and we are from the Bordeaux region. They owned the Chateau Margaux property. There the family produced very good wines. It is said Thomas Jefferson, while visiting the chateau, praised the wine. The property has an incredible history", she went on. "The winery was once owned by Elie du Barry, who was Madame du Barry's brother-in-law. She went to the guillotine for being Louis XV's mistress. It is said she cried, 'Oh, I'll miss the cup of wine I always have before dinner.' Elie was also guillotined."

"What a horrible death!" I blurted.

"Indeed. Those were other times. It was an improvement over the ax, at least. Now heads don't roll, not here, anyway", she said reflectively.

"Well, perhaps just metaphorically." I asserted. She told me the story of how the chateau had changed ownership several times and twice procured by Spanish aristocrats. One was the Marquis de la Colonilla. He had the manor house there replaced with the magnificent chateau which still stands today. But the Marquis liked to live in Paris and never saw the finished product. "What happened to the property then?", I remarked curiously.

"The property was sold in the 1850s to the Marquis de la Marismas, who was also a Spaniard and a friend of my clan. He and his family used the chateau, which is regal, as their permanent home, although he had other estates. He loved the area and had a deep interest in its wines".

"It all sounds riveting", I said.

"You know", Margaux said, "I'm thinking that perhaps we should go to Bordeaux and visit the chateau. I have not been in the area in years."

"Well, it's an excellent idea. Maybe Scott would also enjoy the ride, perhaps he could be our chauffeur", I said, "he has many stories to share."

"That will be fun, but I know he has a busy schedule and something always comes up. Let's not count on it", she warned me.

Chateau Margaux. Early in the morning a week later, we took an overnight trip to Chateau Margaux. The place was breathtaking. There we found a stately pavilion located in the Bordeaux wine region of southwestern France. The wine tour of the premises was outstanding, and had some photos taken by a nice tour guide; later we had lunch. This included a starter, main dish — I had lamb, she had fish — and wine was served, of course. At the end of our meal, we had coffee. Under Margaux's, advice I tried *cannelé*, which is a small French pastry flavored with rum and vanilla. It has a soft and tender custard center and a dark, thick caramelized crust. In one word: scrumptious.

It was a fabulous trip. I learned about wines and mouth-watering French dishes. On our way back Margaux shared a curious tale of how Ernest Hemingway's granddaughter, whose birth name was Margot (1954-1996), changed it to Margaux to match the name of the wine her father, Jack, loved. Supposedly, her father and mother drank from a good vintage the night she was conceived.

Young and curious. I continued to visit the sights with my cousin for a few more days, but she had to go back home. It was then my school friends finally arrived, but continued their trip to Belgium, where they were supposed to stay with friends. They invited me to go along, but I wanted to stay put in Paris. In any case, I had classes to attend.

The following weeks I went out several times with Margaux and sometimes Scott would tag along. They took me to restaurants away from the tourist crowds. She kept telling stories about her family and her experiences traveling with her husband. They had even gone to Russia and China in the days it was not a popular destination. I tried to crank up Scott to talk about his travels, but still, he would clam up. Although he was very open about his project and showed us many of the photos he had already taken, he was also guarded about his personal life. Unnecessarily so for an American, although friendly, it could be said he was too reserved about his profession. After all, we had become friends, at least in my opinion. Likewise, Margaux said Scott had a very private life she had never been able to unravel.

Because she was enthusiastic about touring and her company refreshing and enjoyable, I showed Margaux a list of places to visit, among them small museums and some writers' homes—Paris is filled with them. Always curious about how writers and artists lived, I'm convinced it says a great deal about the person. For example, the furniture they used, the artwork they bought, even the books they read. My new friend examined the list and agreed we could go and visit **Victor Hugo**'s (1802-1885) house.

The museum is located in his former apartment in the heart of the Marais area, at the elegant 6 Place des Vosges. He lived at this address from 1832 to 1848. It is where he wrote many of his famous works, including *The*

Hunchback of Notre-Dame and *Les Miserables*. Although he rented at many other places while in and out of exile during the political crises he lived, this museum gathers his belongings collected by his descendants. I was impressed by the rooms, faithfully recreated, filled with furniture and art that once belonged to Hugo. Even a Sevres vase, gifted by the government, was there. We saw the small bed where he died — he must have been a short man. Also there we found the famous raised desk where he wrote standing up and the many other pieces of furniture he used. We were taken by the dining room with its beautiful chandeliers and period furniture. Among his friends was **Alexandre Dumas** (1802-1870), who wrote *The Three Musketeers* and *The Count of Monte Cristo*.

From Hugo's museum, we continued to **Honoré de Balzac's** (1799-1850) house, in rue Raynouard, which is also a museum. It's a modest residence with a courtyard and a small garden from where we could see the Eiffel Tower. Here is where he wrote many of his best novels including, *La Comedie Humaine* and *La Cousine Bette*. Although most of his furniture is now gone, we were able to see his writing desk, chair and turquoise studded cane. Also drawings of Balzac, of Balzac's mother, an oil portrait of his father, and 19th Century prints of caricaturist and sculptor Honoré Daumier (1808-1879). It was exciting to find a library on the ground floor with the author's original manuscripts, volumes containing his explanatory notes, books signed by him, and magazines of the period. To be among a writer's personal belongings is moving and makes one feels as if we were friends.

Sightseeing with Marla. While active in my classes, I also persisted in my quest of visiting beautiful sites and taking photos everywhere. Plans were made to travel to Fontainebleau and see the palace and then visit Barbizon, the artist's colony. I invited Scott and also my friend Marla, who was visiting Paris, to come along. It was no small wonder when bumping into her at the Jeu de Paume a few days before. Who would have known? I was truly blown away and delighted to see her there. But then again, in Paris, like in Barcelona's Las Ramblas, as Hortensia used to say, the most amazing things can happen. We decided it would be a good idea for her to join me on the outing. She explained she was on her way home after having spent a year in Spain as an English teacher in a private school, but had traveled to Paris to visit the museums.

Scott had already said he was driving to Fontainebleau to drop off a few catalogs. He was to meet a friend who was supposed to travel with him on his next photo shoot. Because now he had a car—borrowed from a buddy—I asked him if coming along with a female friend was a problem. He just said, "no sweat, sure", and that was it. It's always fun to have a guy as an escort, that way if we were to get into trouble with anything which might come up, most of all with the language, he could come to the rescue.

We picked Marla up on a chilly and pleasant civil dawn. The sky had its *l'heure bleue* and the sun was ready just below the horizon. No rain in sight, my mind read. The ride was a breeze. We were finally in Fontainebleau and I was truly excited. The company and the trip had been magical as we laughed and told stories about our experiences traveling. And Marla, who was supposed to be very particular about men, to my surprise, seemed to like Scott.

At the town of Fontainebleau, we met with Scott's friend, Daniel, who had brought along two ladies, Kristina and Nicole. They looked young, and neither of them was married to him, for Scott had mentioned he was married to a woman from Belgium who was in her forties. Knowing the purported habits of some French males—

similar to the Spaniards—the scene with the pretty girls didn't surprise us.[10]

Fontainebleau is a small village located in the middle of a forest where the famous and arresting palace is. Both the former royal residence and little burg are splendid. We arrived in the morning and, once there, decided to visit the palace and its grounds before walking through town. When sightseeing the chateau, with its elegant rooms, furniture, paintings and sculptures, one learns that, starting in the 1500s, the place had been used and remodeled by various royal families up to Napoleon's time, giving it an eclectic look, but nevertheless harmonious. For example, the Trinity Chapel is small but lovely, with a magnificent painted ceiling. Francois I (1494-1547) was the one who built the chapel, and many important events during the monarchies of France took place in this particular location. For instance, the marriage of Louis XV in 1725, the signing of Napoleon's first abdication in 1814, and the baptism of his nephew—who would become Napoleon III.[11]

I fell in love with Fontainebleau palace. It was one of Napoleon's favorite residences. He loved to take long walks in the nearby forest, and that was exactly what we were planning to do.

Before the palace, there was first a hunting lodge and later a country house used from the times of the Capet kings subsequent to the 11th Century. It was here, close to 44 miles from Paris, where various royal family members, starting with Phillip I (the Amorous c.1052-1108), came to vacation. He brought along his wife in bigamy, the beautiful Bertrade de Montfort. The building was later transformed in the 16th Century by Francis I. He expanded and embellished the structure to entertain Anne, a duchess and his mistress. It was their permanent residence on grounds surrounded by a forest. Thirty-four royals, up to and including Napoleon III, enjoyed the place.

Although there are no royals in my family, I felt like one of them after being given the chance of walking around and enjoying everything, including the breathtaking grounds. Nowadays, because of its easy access, gorgeous forest with wild plants and trees, birds, mammals, and butterflies, it's a favorite of Parisians and tourists alike. A getaway to relax with the family or lover, and enjoy nature.

I took pictures of swans, ducks, and children who kept chasing the fowl. Because tourists were scarce, it was as if we owned the place. At the palace store, I bought some books and a lovely, blue demitasse cup decorated with the palace's view and grounds. Being there gave me a sense of privilege.

Fontainebleau was also mired in a tragic story. The Marchese Monaldeschi, the not-so-secret lover of Christina, Queen of Sweden, had, supposedly, betrayed her. In 1657, while they were staying as guests at the Palace, she had him killed in front of her. There was even some chasing after Monaldechi while he bled all over the place. Writers have called her footloose, strong-willed, mischief-maker and unpredictable imp. Also known to be a spendthrift, she was hated everywhere she went.

Barbizon. After touring the palace, its gardens and, putting my camera away, we decided—including Daniel and the girls—to continue to nearby Barbizon. Visiting the quaint, little town had been a dream of mine. I shared my idea with the group and of course Scott said "phenomenal"; the rest thought it would be terrific.

Marla wanted to drive, but Scott took over the wheel once more. He said she wasn't used to driving in Europe and that it could be dangerous. His reasoning seemed absurd and contrary to what we thought we knew. Although Marla was quite an independent person, she agreed and sat next to him. I again wondered if a romance was brewing. A little older than me and already a recent college graduate, she was the one falling in love every week. Driving through the center of town, we stopped at a mouth-watering market and a *patisserie* next door to get some food and also desserts.

Because the Impressionists turned painting outdoors—*en plein air*—into a popular venue, those who follow the movement are aware of all those locations the artists visited and the scenes they painted everywhere they gathered, especially in that little colony of Barbizon. I've always enjoyed looking at *Le déjeuner sur l'herbe [Luncheon on the Grass]*, by Manet. He made his preparatory renderings at the forest in Barbizon. It is a painting so refreshing and relaxing that, the first time I saw it, I promised myself someday to have a picnic there to recreate it as a tableau vivant. And that wish finally came true. Of course, we didn't strip for the picnic. It was more in the style of *Luncheon on the Grass* by Claude Monet.

Daniel bought bottles of white wine, a bottle of Evian for me, and a bottle of champagne to accompany the desserts, which were of different types, but mainly combinations with chocolate. We all craved them.

It was still early. We walked around the lovely little town to feel the ambiance. Because spring was just beginning, mostly locals walking dogs or jogging were roving around. There was, however, something of a curiosity that made us laugh, the sight of a well-dressed grandmother walking a cat on a leash. The French are odd and funny that way, even if they don't see each other in that light. Anything offbeat can be expected.

The village was almost deserted. The merchants—with nothing to do—were delighted to see us as they showed ample smiles of welcome. Could it be a new phenomenon?, we commented. What could have altered or influenced the change? In any case, we were amused, for it was not the Parisian world we were accustomed to.

As we kept looking here and there, Marla said, "Is there anything else to do in this part of the world besides the palace and shops?"

"Yeah, I know someone who rents horses", Daniel replied.

"I love it!" I cut in before he could completely exhale.

"Hold it, hold it", said Scott. "Don't think you can gallop through town like in a western".

"Don't be silly", I complained. "Just a wholesome walk through this beautiful forest that surrounds us." It didn't take long for all of us to sit on a saddle and softly steer beautiful equine specimens down a well-traveled path among the trees. The smell of sweating horses and tree bark brought back memories of my childhood; I quivered.

Along the way we found other riders coming out of the forest who waved as we pass them by.

"J'adore cet endroit" [I love this place], one of them yelled. The lesson learned is how important it is to know people well-acquainted with an area. As we rode, we also saw hikers with backpacks moving through the abundant and rare rock formations found in the park.

Having returned the horses to the stable, we sat on the grass to relax and engage in animated conversation. With hovering trees, the ground was covered with wild-flowers and dry leaves, making it a picturesque scene. The bread tasty and crisp, pungent cheeses of every kind, soft and creamy pâtés, fruits and the mouth-watering desserts made it look like the tableaux vivant I envisioned.

With Marla still imbibing the last drops of wine, Scott got up, excused himself, and went walking with Daniel, who was holding a rather large piece of chocolate. They left us with the two mademoiselles whose proficiency in English was worse than ours in French. It was fun to practice our "patois" as we laid on the grass under shady trees and a blue sky. We laughed and shared ideas; this was la *vie en rose*.

When the guys came back, I realized Scott had disappeared with his briefcase for at least half an hour. Wondering what it was he was doing that was so important he could not do it around us, I decided to mind my own business and respect his privacy. Pouring himself some more wine, Scott sat by Marla and me, staying away from Daniel's girls. The sun was getting warm and the two female visitors decided to remove their blouses to take the sunshine. They were not wearing bras. Scott shook his head with a broad smile, Marla mentioned that even in Spain they are doing it all over the beaches, and I, leaning on Scott, whispered, "you won't see that back home"

"*C'est la vie*", he responded while looking at *les jeunes femmes*. The rascal was having a good time with gratuitous entertainment.

The day had gone swiftly, and experiencing such a beautiful place made my day. It got dark quickly as we rushed from the forest to find a place to stay in the village of Barbizon; the wine had gone down fast and the guys were not ready to drive back. I called Margaux to let her know not to expect me till the next day, and she understood. Mentioning we were having a great time, I told her about my picture-taking and my love for the palace and the quaintness of the small town. So much so that the place claimed me forever.

The hotel where we spent the night in Barbizon is located at the edge of the forest and had a lovely view. The French girls also decided to stay and we all four slept in the same room. Scott and his friend shared another. By then, tired and hungry, we decided to eat right at the hotel, having had enough adventures for the day. The moon was full and the evening had a pleasant chill, but not cold. We asked to seat outside. The two girls with Daniel decided to walk to a petite restaurant they spotted earlier. Daniel, in a flirting mood, had other plans. I just articulated, "*amusez vous bien!*" [have a great time.]

The restaurant at the hotel was inviting and the service pleasant. I had a delicious gourmet dinner of *potau-feu*, which is boiled beef and vegetables seasoned the way only the French can. Scott and Marla asked for *coq au vin*, and we all finished dinner with an apple *tarte Tatin*. The whole experience was beyond yummy. Turning in early, we slept like logs.

At breakfast, butter was king, as it always is in France. It was scrumptiously palate-pleasing. Scott and Daniel said they still had a few more things to do around the area and, upon that, Kristina and Nicole invited us to see the competitions at the *Haras des Brulys* in Barbizon. On that day, as luck would have it, according to the program, Princess Grace of Monaco,[12] former actress Grace Kelly, was supposed to be there to present an award. But to me, what was thrilling was being around those gorgeous horses, given that, as a child, my grandfather spoiled me with a colt on my birthday. Finally we spotted Grace, and realized she was as poised and pretty as she appeared in her films.

The competition was exciting and the horses, of various colors, had a stunning presence.

After walking around the stables, at my insistence to see other magnificent equine specimens, we went back to the hotel. An hour later, standing on the sidewalk, we said goodbye to Kristina and Nicole.

At a distance, we saw Scott waving and walking briskly toward us after apparently finishing his dealings in the area. Soon we were on our way.

"Ok, Scott, what now?" I said whimsically.

"Well, I'll be free for a few days. We can make another stop. What the heck...", he answered.

"We could pay a visit to the town where Colette was born", I said optimistically. "I believe it's pronounced Saint-Sauveur-en-Puisaye. Did I say it right?"

"Close enough", he said laughing. "That's the lady who wrote Gigi, right?"

"Yep", I said.

"Well, it's due south about 60 miles as the crow flies", he replied.

"Right!", said Marla. "But we are not crows and we travel by car. How long does it take to get there?"

"Less than an hour and a half with normal traffic", he answered.

And off we went heading south. We took our time getting there, steering through little detours, and stopping along the way to enjoy the scenery and take some pics. Seeing that Scott was a good driver, I felt secure and relaxed. Apparently, he felt talkative as he began to share his experiences and childhood stories. He told us how he had traveled all over France, enjoying the countryside as a child. His parents, especially his mother who was a professor, were curious about learning the country's different regions, people, temperaments and their influences on France as a whole. I thought about his anecdotes and felt a kinship. I also had the same thirst for adventure and knowledge about people, local customs and society in general.

As we trekked through the small towns, past farms, and talked to locals, I noticed changes in friendliness. Some engaged us in conversation, others kept to themselves or ignored us completely. But it is in the big cities where we find the most discourteous people in general. Now even Marla, after we left Barbizon, was thinking of staying in France longer, but in a small town close to Paris, where she could get a job teaching English. I was glad she told us, for, in need of a social friend for other little trips around Paris, we made a good team. The sharing of adventures was always on my mind. There is so much to see in France beyond Paris. Although I suspected there was more to her decision about not leaving lovely Paris right away, noticing, one more time, she positioned herself close to Scott; however, he seemed friendly but aloof towards her.

Colette. I told Scott it would be terrible for me to walk away from this part of the country without visiting Colette's hometown while I had the chance. An experience like no other for an admirer of the writer, especially because she was penning at a time when it was hard for a woman to be published and be taken seriously. Nevertheless, college savants still don't think too highly of her output.

Sidonie-Gabrielle Colette (1873-1954)[13] was born in St-Sauveur-en-Puisaye, a small village on the side of a hill overlooking the fertile plains of central France; a farmtown with few streets and no traffic lights, where she spent the first seventeen years of her life.

On the trip there, along the way we discovered placid golden ponds decorating the landscape, birds, butterflies and wild rabbits. Because I love rolling hills, medieval cities, and the bewitchment of the laid-back atmosphere of ancient constructions, the place enthralled me. When we got to the village, it reminded us of the perfect spot to dream of bygone days. The sky was a soft blue and there was a pleasant breeze coming from the south. Lucky to revel in Scott's and Marla's fun-loving attitude, and that she wanted to experience life in France, I realized my reservations about traveling without my school friends were nonsense.

Colette's Burgundian village has a beautiful storybook landscape with forests filled with ineffable castles. We could see signs everywhere with her name identifying that lovely place as her own. The first thing we spotted was the house where she was born. The abode was privately owned and not open to the public, but one could recognize the two-story, 17th Century stone house and garden from the description in her novels. And there is a sign on the house that lets you know you have arrived where she was born. After reading some of her books, I definitely wanted to visit her, if only spiritually, and see where this author was born and how she was inspired by her surroundings. And once you're there it's easy to decipher where her ideas originated, especially those in her first books, the Claudine stories. Finally we can understand where the feelings she poured into her writings came from.

To be in Colette's hamlet had been a dream of mine. The lovely and talented Sidonie-Gabrielle, perhaps because she lived in a captivating part of France, was blessed with an active imagination. No doubt she had a stimulating life as a young child and later, even more so, as an adult. Reading about her life, which was interesting, to say the least, taught me she had lived in that pretty community all her young life.

As a blossoming *mademoiselle*, she met Henry Gauthier-Villars, fourteen years her senior. He had fallen in love with her and, as she turned twenty, became her first husband in 1893.

While reading about her life, it is effortless to capture that she probably tied the knot because her village was becoming too small for her and Henry, who was a writer and music critic. It was after they wedded that the two moved to Paris looking for a broader audience. Colette never went back to live in Burgundy.

Once they settled in the big city, she caught on about Henry's many contacts with writers and artists in the bohemian world, but also, more or less, she discovered his promiscuous lifestyle while introducing her to the intellectual and avant-garde circles; eventually, even encouraging her to have lesbian affairs. Henry, who was a slick operator, owned the copyrights to her *Claudine* series and was also shown as co-author—his name was removed from later editions—of the works. As she matured, realizing she was being used, and tired of his amorous liaisons, by 1906 she dropped him. Unable to earn a living, she lodged with a variety of friends and had several flings herself, some quite scandalous.

Henry had accustomed Colette to live an unfettered sexual lifestyle and she accepted it. We would never know whether she did it out of convenience or the fear that she couldn't make it on her own. With no shame after walking away from Henry, her life took an unusual turn. Her behavior and personality seemed to be at odds with the morals of the time, even for a maverick. Her mindset was risque then as it would be now. Needing some earnings, she then threw herself into the cabaret life, appearing in many clubs and acting in shows. She emerged naked at the Moulin Rouge in *An Egyptian Dream*[14] with the sculptor and aristocrat, Marquise Mathilde de Morny. It seems she might have been using all the experiences to later write her stories, as many writers do. The title, *The Pure and the Impure*, seems to be inspired by those affairs. After a few years of excess, always in need, it was then she became a journalist, often writing about the decadent Parisian social world she now knew so well. No doubt she was quite an oddity and proved to be emancipated for her times. She lived life with great excitement and squeezed every drop of joy she could, doing what she thought was right for her; no one else mattered.

By 1912 she eloped and married another Henry, Henri de Jouvenel des Ursins; perhaps another marriage of convenience. He was the editor of *Le Matin*, a newspaper to which she was a contributor. In July 1913, they had a daughter she also named Colette. But she continued to be restless, supposedly having an affair with her sixteen-year-old stepson, Bertrand de Jouvenel, and, because of this relationship, by 1924 Henri divorced her.

But Colette was not content living alone, and in 1925 she married her last husband, Maurice Goudeket, a pearl salesman who was many years her junior. By then she was an established novelist. Colette supported him financially and they remained together till her death at their apartment in the Palais Royal. People knew where she lived, and many would linger to see her sitting by the window in a wheelchair when she was no longer able to leave the house because of her chronic rheumatism. She was a positive person, liked to watch people go by, see friends, and enjoyed what she could see of the Paris she loved. Jean Cocteau, the writer and filmmaker, was one of those soul-mates — and neighbor at Palais Royale — who would visit her. She wrote from her early 20s to her 70s. Through her writings, we get a deep sense of delight and the crazy occasions enjoyed by the bohemian cafe society of the age. Colette was a successful author in her time and her work was semi-autobiographical, intimate and colorful, and although she wrote many books, it's Gigi, the 1958 film with Leslie Caron, that attracted me to her other works.

It had been an unforgettable trip to her village. After walking around the hamlet for an hour, we left St-Sauveur-en-Puisaye and went back to Paris. The small town was everything I expected, except there was no museum dedicated to her at the time.[15] Nevertheless, by visiting her town and the roads she had strolled in her childhood, I was closer to her and knew more about this unique author and woman than what I had read in books.

My wanderlust rolls on. On the road for a while, we were famished and went looking for a place to eat. We felt happy to find a pleasant little bistro along the way serving healthy food. There we enjoyed the asparagus

Auguste Renoir

Georges Braque

Raoul Duffy

Maurice Utrillo and his
mother, Suzanne Valadon

The hues of Aix de Provance

Cezanne studs guide

Renoir's *Bal du moulin de la Galette*. Dancing in the middle distance (left) is Cuban painter Don Pedro Vidal de Solares y Cárdenas, with the model Margot

Renoir's *Luncheon of the Boating Party*

Picasso's *Les Demoiselles d'Avignon*

Gustave Moreau

Edgar Degas

Josephine Baker and her
paramour Le Corbusier

The Noveau district at Montmarte

George Sand

Musee of the vie Romantique

Gustave Moreau museum

Interior of Basilica Sacre Coeur

de Gas (Degas) mausoleum. Montmartre Cemetery

St. Pierre church in Montmarte

Moulin de la Galette

The author at Chopin's tomb in Père Lachaise cemetery

The author at the bookstore

Cézanne's *The Card Players*

August Rodin   Rodin Museum

Camille Claudel

Hotel where we stayed at Aix de Provence

Jas de Bouffan, Cézanne's home

Mont Sainte-Victoire by Cézanne

Mont Sainte-Victoire

94

The author in the spring

Le Bon Bock

Guillerme Appolinaire

The author at the Montmartre Museum

Henri de Toulouse-Lautrec

Poster by Toulouse-Lautrec

The author and Iolanda at Sacred Heart

chicken with red pepper sauce, veal in a mushroom cream sauce with broiled garlic accompanied with artichokes, and green peppers soaked in brandy. We shared the servings for each to have a taste of the different dishes. Scott ordered a bottle of a local Bourgogne Chardonnay that he said was amazing and shared it with Marla. As always, I asked for a glass of Evian with lemon wedges. It was a fun and delicious experience. To finish it off we had espressos to stay awake while driving through France's treacherous back roads.

Because we took the long way and scenic route to get back to Paris—at my insistence—it was already getting dark by the time we got to the center of the city. Once we got to Margaux's place she invited us to share some crepes filled with ham and gruyere cheese, together with a perfectly seasoned salad of lettuce, green beans, asparagus, celery, almonds and green apples dressed with lemon mayonnaise. It was exquisite. Margaux and I had tea, Scott and Marla, wine. I told her all about our excursion, what we saw and the experiences with Daniel's mademoiselles in Barbizon. We all laughed. "Here in France", she explained, "everyone goes topless while sunbathing."

When we finished dessert, a fabulous Napoleon covered with powdered coffee and accompanied by espresso, I announced the notion of returning to Montmartre the next day, after my art class, to take some photographs and to visit certain intriguing homes where artists once lived. Marla begged off because she wanted to visit a friend outside of Paris, Scott had to work in one of those unintelligible projects nobody could understand, and Margaux said she was expecting a friend from Madrid. In other words, I would be on my own again.

Montmartre was not new to me, for Scott had taken me around the hip place the first night we met. Excited, on waking up the next morning, I threw a blouse and a pair of socks in my backpack in case I decided to stay overnight—the temperature was still a bit cool—and also brought along cheese, bread, and bars of dark chocolate. Then, after my class, I took a metro ride to the most exciting place in Paris—at least to me.

Montmartre. In the 18th arrondissement, this district, dating to Roman times, was built on a hill at the northern edge of the city and is part of the Right Bank. I wanted to feel like the locals and walk the walk artists followed.

There are a bunch of small hotels near rue des Abbesses, where my school friends had stayed before, and the subway station is nearby. In case I changed my mind, I didn't make a reservation. In that district you could also find some good restaurants, crepe stands and cafes. I could easily do sightseeing at night as long as I stayed away from Pigalle, the red light sector.

Museum of Montmartre. Once there, my own tour began. Map in hand, I took rue St. Vincent, which led to the Museum of Montmartre at 12 rue Cortot. Long ago, in this district, you could stumble upon the elusive van Gogh or Renoir. One could run into Le Corbusier or Picasso's colleague, Georges Braque, Cubism in his mind and under his arm. Or one could sit and chat with Raoul Duffy, a Fauve artist, and with Henri Matisse or Edgar Degas while enjoying a drink. The rent in Montmartre was modest in those days, and painters, as was always the case, seldom had enough money to buy brushes. Many stayed in the village until they began to get recognized. A good example of this was Picasso, whose work was in demand as early as 1909 at the age of twenty-eight, something that was seldom the case.

The museum is truly a small gem. It is a good idea to visit it first and then later relax while strolling around the neighborhood. The building is one of the oldest in the area and it is easily missed if you don't probe for secluded surprises. Many painters had studios in what is now the museum, such as Maurice Utrillo (1883-1955)—with his mother, Suzanne Valadon (1865-1938), who was also a painter—and Auguste Renoir (1841-1919), who lived and worked there. At this place, you can as well enjoy the artwork of many artists which recount the history of Montmartre and its cabarets, including that of the Moulin Rouge—still kicking high for the can-can a few blocks away. Likewise, in the museum there is a room dedicated to that chorus line dance made famous by the females in Henri de Toulouse-Lautrec's (1864-1901) many posters, with his cabaret and bohemian-inspired themes. To my surprise, there were some rarely seen, evoking that bygone era. I enjoyed looking at the *Le Lapin Agile* painting and coming across *Le Chat Noir* poster. Le Chat, to many the first modern nightclub, had been a popular literary and artistic cabaret, where the creative young people of *fin de siècle* Paris gathered to partake and be entertained. In the museum, there were no guides but a guard, an older and very sweet gentleman with a large mustache. He was helpful, pleasant and coquettish like most French men are. He didn't care if I spoke a word of French. He took me by the hand and guided me to the window to look outside and see one of Montmartre's last surviving vineyards.[16]

Clos Montmartre. It was a thrilling surprise. The small vineyard is on Rue Saint-Vincent and lends its hole-in-the-wall existence to local efforts to keep Montmartre unique in the highly urbanized *Île de France* region.

After touring the small but captivating museum, I dropped by their tiny store and bought several miniature pink glasses with a design of *le Chat Noir* to give to Margaux as a gift, although she probably had one already.

Around lunchtime, hungry and before leaving, I visited the museum's courtyard and garden and sat on a bench. After a little prayer to give thanks for having been able to make the trip, even without my schoolmates, I savored my small lunch, relaxed, and contemplated the moment among so much history, together with a black cat that was hiding among the flowers. I had the impression Renoir and all his pals were around me smiling. While in the garden I struck up a conversation with a young couple visiting from Italy, Flora and Giancarlo. Their French was as bad as their English, but we were able to understand each other with my Italian from high school and native Spanish, which was close enough. They had come to Paris to tie the knot in front of the Eiffel Tower, a dream of theirs since the day they got engaged.

Art and architecture students in Florence, a friend had offered them his apartment in Paris while he was away in business. The idea of the nuptials was quite romantic, and, as we sat on the bench, I offered them slices of cheese. We shared like old friends and they explained it would have been hard for the families to make it from Tuscany, but the lovebirds assured me they were planning a second ceremony at their neighborhood chapel near Siena. Because they noticed I was taking photographs, they asked me if I would mind meeting them at the tower and take a few pics. In a heartbeat I said "Yes!" — another adventure.

Their idea sounded exciting. How could I refuse, they were gorgeous and totally smitten with each other. We made plans to meet, and then asked them to come along for a walk around the borough. Looking for other sights, we came across marvelous cobblestone roads and old houses. I kept clicking away.

There is a lot to see in this small district. I'd read about a building called Le Bateau-Lavoir, so named because the wood construction was old and made a creaking sound—like boats do—during stormy nights as the structure settled in its hilly surroundings. I found it at No. 13 Rue Ravignan, close to the Place du Terre, the square where painters still gather to sell their work. Sadly, the building burned down, and only the storefront was left standing. At one time Le Bateau-Lavoir was a residence and also a kind of club for many early 20th Century artists, writers and art dealers who were forever looking to discover new talent. While there, Picasso[17] painted one of his most famous work, *Les Demoiselles d'Avignon*—a forerunner of cubism and modern art—where five prostitutes from the back streets of Barri Gotic of Barcelona plied their trade.

This village was also home to Degas, who lived and died at No 6 Boulevard de Clichy, and Picasso, who lived for a while at No 11. However, at the beginning of World War I, artists began moving to Montparnasse (Mount Parnassus), a former hill—flattened in the 18th Century, where two hundred years before students went to recite poetry to the inspirational goddess of literature—about five miles to the south on the left bank, which they could now afford.

But as some artists moved away from Montmartre, others took their place, and by 1928 Studio 28 opened as the first cinema in the world for experimental films.[18] Also writers, dancers and singers continued the lively scene at this hilly district, including entertainer Josephine Baker[19] and her paramour, Swiss architect Le Corbusier, at the artistic salon R2613—at 26 Rue Norvins. Here the bohemian atmosphere was king. A perfect scenario not only for painters and musicians, but also for authors like Jean Cocteau, Gertrude Stein and her companion, Alice.

In this marvelous village, we found narrow alleys with ivy-clad houses as we walked to the foot of Montmartre, just south of Pigalle, to the quarter of Nouvelle

Athenes—named after the neoclassical miniature mansions—built in the 19th century.

My new soon-to-be-wed friends kept stopping once in a while to kiss. As I pointed to where painter Paul Delaroche once lived at Rue St. Lazare 58, I looked back, but they weren't listening. At Rue de la Rochefoucauld we found the Musée Gustave Moreau, where we were able to snoop around the artist's apartment and studio. Then, walking north, also on Nouvelle Athenes at 16 rue Chaptal, we came across an interesting museum.

Musée de la Vie Romantique. This place is one of the many literary museums found in Paris. It has a greenhouse, a courtyard and a lovely rose garden that was beginning to bloom when we were there. In 1830 this was the private residence of Dutch painter Ary Scheffer, who was close to King Louis-Philippe and his family. The artist and his daughter used to host evening salons[20]among the famous of the day. It was here where Delacroix, Rossini, Franz Liszt, Chopin and the irrepressible George Sand—Aurore Dupin—used to meet. The edifice has two floors. On display you can find George Sands's memorabilia, family portraits, furniture, household possessions, jewels and *objets d'art*. There were as well paintings by Francois Bouchet and sculptures by different artists. But the one of George Sand in marble, by Auguste Clesinger, is remarkable. These museums, together with Maison Victor Hugo and Maison de Balzac, are an inspiration. Anyone who loves literature and art should visit them.

It was now four o'clock and we had enjoyed a terrific time. My new friends were lively and witty, like most Italians I know are. The opportunity to practice Italian vocabulary, including salty expressions, was priceless. I invited them to come along to visit the Sacred Heart Basilica, but they declined. In unison and through laughter they said, "we're tired." Looking at each other they continued, "we want to go back to our place." After kisses and hugs, they left, and I went to a small shop and bought a bottle of sparkling cider and cheese, to slowly consume while trekking uphill towards the basilica.

The view from the top. Scott had mentioned the view of Paris from the top of Montmartre was breathtaking. At the corner of rue Véron, a musician was playing old songs on an accordion. The gentleman was so articulate and amusing that it lured me to contribute to his hat. Continuing up the steps running parallel to the *funiculaire*, I ran into and joined two girls from Portugal who were visiting for a few days and shared my ideas. They were sisters, Catia and Iolanda.

The splendid thing about being a visitor in a foreign land is that you will find lots of people traveling alone or in small groups who are ready to mingle and fraternize.

We kept on climbing to the Basilica, and, turning around, I realized Scott was right. It is the best place from where to see Paris. Gazing up next to the church, the imposing white-domed of the edifice gave me goosebumps. Because the Sacré-Coeur was built on the second highest hill of Paris—the top observation point of the Eiffel is the tallest, however—the full panorama is perfect to behold. We sat to admire the scenery and waited till dusk to see the reflections of the red clouds. They were stunning.

It was an energizing moment to share soft drinks and the girls singing Edith Piaf's[21] songs. I even got an invitation to visit Portugal. Before the night was over, we resolved to go the next day to Pere Lachaise cemetery, where the famous and notorious are buried. What a terrific time we had. I decided to stay with them and called Margaux and Gloria to let them know, then the three of us had dinner at a cute bistro. After a heartfelt *bon nuit*, we turned in.

Getting up early, I popped into the same bistro we had enjoyed the night before, ordered a *café au lait* — like I'd done back home — and a croissant, before walking to Saint-Pierre de Montmartre at Place des Abbesses, 2 rue du Mont Cenis. Visiting churches is a side interest of mine that I learned from Hortensia on this trip; they give me a sense of serenity to clear my thoughts and help me continue with my projects. Because fewer tourists visit Saint-Pierre, it is more relaxing than Sacre-Coeur. At the smaller church, you can meditate peacefully. Different from most religious buildings, its red facade is simple and unassuming, but inside it has the old, high and long nave of Gothic architecture. I stayed there for a while taking in the peacefulness of the place.

Montmartre cemetery. The girls had agreed to meet me after breakfast at the entrance of the cemetery. With 20,000 burial plots, there are many famous people buried here. Alexander Dumas, Edgar Degas, Vaslav Nijinsky, Stendhal, and Émile Zola. The list is long and it includes famous scientists, philosophers and politicians.

We stayed together all morning while walking around the village and Boulevard de Clichy. Then took photos at 6 rue de l'Abreuvoir hoping to see Renoir's ghost in the prints, and continued to 54 Rue Lepic, where Vincent van Gogh stayed with his brother, Theo, in an apartment on the third floor.

But this district is more than just a beautiful postcard from the past. It's still alive and well. Moreover, we decided to do some exploring off the usual track everyone visits, for a glimpse of the real Montmartre. Strolling around Place des Abbesses to find rustic houses and very narrow roads — that escaped the design and urban renewal of Baron Haussmann — was a thrill. This part seems to be what Paris looked like before urban renewal. Until 1860, this area was a separate village with windmills all around, of which only two survived, the Radet 83, Rue Lepic, and the Blute-Fin at the corner of Rue Girardon. Together they are part of the grounds of the famous Moulin de la Galette, immortalized by Renoir, Van Gogh—twice—and Toulouse-Lautrec.

We finished our little tour at a small diner, where we paused for a light lunch and coffee. The girls were delightful and funny and we decided to practice our French with the waitress.

She was probably in her 50s and, given that our pronunciation was terrible, the lady kept making faces of disapproval. The woman couldn't decipher what we were ordering, but she was no help, either. Being young and in a light mood, we began to laugh. The server was not amused. We thought it must be stress. Because the lady spoke some English, she told us to order that way; however, her English wasn't better than our French. But her insistence didn't deter us. Wanting to practice French, we made an effort and spoke slowly; ultimately we were served. Once finished with the meal, she came back with the check before we asked for it, something not typical of French restaurants. However, given that the tip is included in the bill—as I mentioned before—the rascal knew it would not affect her gratuity. Already infused with laughter, we left the restaurant still giggling. I told the girls servers behave differently outside the big cities. Margaux had mentioned it, and she also felt the problem was the amount of work they had and what they were paid. Perhaps, but the only big city I had come across with that nonchalant attitude is Paris. Although, in the spirit of fairness, servers in museum eateries were kind—maybe influenced by the environment. Thank God the city has a lot to offer and people are willing to visit and put up with it.

Exiting, we walked to the bottom of the hill to Place Blanche, where the Moulin Rouge is located. Happy with my new friends and the hilarious situation we had just experienced, we sure had a fantastic time. Those are the simple things in life we never forget.

Pere Lachaise cemetery. After finishing our sightseeing in Montmartre, and following the "dearly departed" procession, we decided to continue to Pere Lachaise cemetery. Although many prominent people are buried there also, we particularly wanted to visit Edith Piaf's and Frédéric Chopin's grave.

By early afternoon we bid adieu and parted, but not before we exchanged addresses and promised to visit each other.

Upon returning to Margaux's, and sharing with her my recent experiences, she mentioned Scott would be dropping by for dinner and I offered to make a Spanish omelet. One of those that is two inches thick in a mixture of onions, fried potatoes—and about anything else you fancy to throw in—with beaten eggs fried the way my mother taught me how to flip so it would cook well on both sides. I didn't dare to prepare anything French, lest my friend could be offended. They are serious and particular about their cuisine the same way they are about their language. Margaux was excited and answered *"oui, oui"* to the idea. She loved anything Spanish. She mentioned how one of the tapas she was served, while visiting her friend in Seville, included a Spanish tortilla mixed with *chorizo* and shoestring fried potatoes. By the time Scott arrived—Margaux already had a few glasses of *vino*—we were practicing *sevillanas*[22] and laughing at silly jokes like teenagers in a sleepover. She was fun!

To accompany my *omelette*, Margaux made a heavenly salad with cucumber, basil, mint leaves, whole scallions, radishes, black olives and cherry tomatoes, dressed with olive oil mixed with Dijon mustard and crushed walnuts on a green oak lettuce bed. All this served with crispy bread she had just bought. The conversation over dinner was reflective and stimulating, with Scott telling us how he had taken some new pics of the homeless from Africa, who were sleeping under a bridge. I said to him, "You see, Scott, although I'm sure your project would be interesting and enlightening, I much rather take beautiful pictures of Paris. I want to make people dream of special moments. A fantasy, like in a Disney film."

"Well, that's fine, that's your line of pollyanna, but someone has to show the other side of the coin. Life is not a rose garden", he retorted.

"True, but life is too short and I enjoy dreaming and sharing fabulous moments. My mission in life is to make people happy. That is why our projects are so different. They are both valid, but contrasting", I countered.

After dinner, Scott invited me to a poetry reading at Shakespeare and Company,[23] an English language bookstore right in the center of Paris near the left bank, a stone-throw away from the cathedral. The poet we went to meet, and whose name escapes me now, was a young man from Holland, and, as coincidence would have it, he was a friend of a friend of Marla, who also happened to be there. Upon seeing Scott, she hastened to sit by his side.

This poet was a student of English literature and was presenting his first book of poetry in English. They served wine and delicious finger snacks. In Paris, one learns to live it up and not count calories. Walking everywhere takes care of your weight — you hope. After the reading, Marla invited us to go with her friend to an all-night jazz session. Scott thought it was a "phenomenal" idea, but I was tired and took a short walk to Margaux's place using the Pont de l'Archevêché and Pont Saint-Louis.

Here comes the bride. I had related to Scott about the nice Italian kids from the museum and to whom I'd promised wedding pictures. He volunteered to come along. Luckily, the morning was crisp with vibrant colors, and although we got there early, they were already waiting for us by the Eiffel Tower. The bride had a light blue, almost white, laced dress she explained had belonged to her favorite aunt. We set up, took the photos and later had them printed. They came out gorgeous. The pair were both good-looking and friendly as you expect many Italian to be. After we finished the shoot, they were so appreciative that, to my surprise, they invited us to join them the next day on a trip to Provence. Particularly the area of Mont Sainte-Victoire—about eight miles from Aix-en-Provence—where Paul Cézanne[24] (1839-1906) spent more than twenty years painting landscapes in and around the place. Being a fan of Cézanne, I agreed to go along and so did Scott. Marla was elated. She had never visited the city and was excited at the prospect. Although Scott had already phoned earlier that he couldn't make it and Marla was disappointed when I told her, she decided to make the trip, anyway.

Morning glory. The Italian newlyweds showed up at the assigned location with two fine-looking young men. One was Italian and the other a French lad from Perpignan, and had met at the building they were staying. Renting a car that looked rather small for a party of six, we all squeezed in and away we went.

The Italian fellow began to sing and we tried to follow playing chorus and clapping our hands. It was terrific traveling with them. They showed a positive attitude and their enthusiasm rubbed off on all of us. Upon getting tired, we would stop for quick espressos at one of the little towns near the highway. Laughing and singing all the way to Mont Sainte-Victoire, the back roads were fun. Because we stopped often, the drive there was long but lovely; snacking at cute bistros along the way as the green countryside encircled us with sunflowers.

Cézanne et moi. Once near Mont Sainte-Victoire, we saw the white cliffs; the ones people have admired so many times in Cézanne's paintings.

In Aix-en-Provence—the locals like to call it *"petit Paris"*—we parked at the edge of the city's center and took a ten-minute walk to its hub. To our great delight, the former Roman village with graceful byways and classic squares radiated a special character. I was aware Cézanne, who died in 1906, traveled the Provence region extensively and had spent more than twenty years painting its landscape. In an instance, we understood the magic and the reason why it not only inspired the post-impressionist Cézanne, but other impressionists and current artists who visit after him. They're all intrigued by the beauty of the countryside. And my camera liked it too, as I captured the charm of the place. This ancient town is surrounded by delightful pink stone walls and fabulous tiled roofs that are bathed, almost year-round, with the unique Provence sun that covers the structures. The majestic mountain contours, with their unusual austere geological forms, change with sunlight according to the time of day. One can truly enjoy a burst of hues not found in a color wheel. We were lucky the number of tourists was small and it didn't take us long to find a place to stay. Hitting upon a lovely hotel near the fountain on the Cours Mirabeau, we decided to check in and then leave to have dinner at a nearby restaurant.

Lacking twenty years like Cézanne to enjoy the scenery, we promenaded around town discovering every niche. My new friends were filled with adventure because, unknown to us, both were art history majors.

The next morning we got up at dawn and found a bakery that served a first-class breakfast, while Marla was showing signs of affection once again, this time towards the Italian fellow. The French guy, who spoke Spanish with an adorable Provençal accent, was delightfully cute and was hanging on my every word—French men can turn flirty in a flash. Beaming, we wanted to walk where Cézanne had walked and, to our surprise, signs about the artist were everywhere, as if he had owned the town. It was easy, the artist's trail is marked with "C" studs. First, we visited his atelier, which he built behind a garden gate after his family estate was sold.

The studio is just north of the town center near the Avenue Paul-Cézanne—of course. It was interesting to discover and recognize, displayed there, many of the objects we had seen in his paintings. On the outskirts of Aix, we also came across the old *Jas de Bouffan* estate, which his father bought in 1859. The Cézannes lived in this house till 1899 when the family sold the property after his mother died. We were able to visit it, but, to our disenchantment, the rooms of this large house were mostly empty. Yet, Cézanne's spirit was felt everywhere on the grounds. The house and its surroundings are represented numerous times in his canvases; his last work within the estate was *The Pool at the Jas de Bouffan* (1888-1890). He was inspired by the impressionists' idea of working outdoors and painting, as they used to say, in *plein* air. These works were filled with light. One piece I've always enjoyed is *The Allée of Chestnut Trees*. In this work, the colors are very refreshing and one can almost feel the country breeze.

Comparing notes on our way back to Paris, I was thrilled knowing we had accomplished more than expected. Cézanne is indeed an inspiration, considering how it took him 30 years of sacrifices and hard work to finally have his first exhibition. It makes us never to think of giving up our quest. Now I was more determined than ever to follow my bliss and someday present my own display of photographs.

My movable feast. Back in Paris, Marla made plans to visit the famous eatery, Brasserie Lipp, having read about it in Hemingway's *A Moveable Feast* (1964). Although I didn't want to stop by the typical touristy places, curiosity made me give in. Not only did Hemingway dined there often, but Picasso, Chagall, Fitzgerald, Simone de Bovier, and Camus were among the many who gathered there. It's quintessential Parisian, and remains a gathering venue for artists, modern intellectuals, politicians and the Paris elite. It was worth dining there, even if for the atmosphere alone. We found it at Boulevard St. Germain in the 6th arrondissement, across Cafe Deux Magots and Café de Flore.

Although all the waiters seemed pleasant, we were lucky to have a Spaniard serving us. Upon entering the place, once they realized we spoke Spanish, he was sent over. His name was Jordi and he was fabulous, as Spanish servers usually are. All smiles, young and nice-looking, he told us he was going to school in Paris. Very knowledgeable, he knew the brasserie's history well. It opened in 1880. The original owners were an Alsatian couple who had left their place of birth when it became part of Germany after the Franco-Prussian War. The decor is very 1920s Art Deco, one of my favorites as far as interior design is concerned. There were mosaics, paintings and also mirrored walls. All the waiters looked elegant, dressed in black and white with bow ties, and long white aprons. Because we were there for a late lunch, not too many customers were teasing their palate.

To see the world go by, we sat close to the door, and, as Hemingway did, ordered potatoes in olive oil, served with deliciously crispy bread. Then we asked for escargots in butter. Marla wanted steak and fries, and I a tuna niçoise salad. We both drank mint tea. Before starting on our way out, Jordi invited us to a party the next day. One good thing about meeting people when you travel: As I mentioned previously, those you come across who are foreigners, seem to be friendlier when they are away from home. Of course, all of us are more amiable the younger we are. Marla said yes right away; she found him irresistible.

It was going to be a bash in honor of a friend who was going back to Madrid. We accepted and joined them to eat the most delicious paella, which Jordi himself prepared. There was a mix of French and Spanish females in attendance, a few witty and funny. Some of the guys were from Seville and we found them to be magnificent specimens: humorous, amusing and handsome. In my opinion, they are the best-looking men in Spain.

After finalizing school in France, Jordi wrote he was going back to Madrid to marry a girl from Seville he had met in school in Paris. Another love story with a happy ending. Paris is like that, forever giving the world romance. Although some years have passed, Marla and I kept in touch with Jordi. After I got married, on one of our trips we dropped by Jordi's parents' home in Madrid, who were very congenial and made us stay for dinner.

The elusive Scott. The following week, my new friends wanted to go to the Louvre, but having been there several times, I decided to go ahead instead with plans Margaux and Scott had made. Scott was supposed to join us with a friend and take us to lunch at Le Bon Bock, but they never showed up. This was odd, I thought. For him not to be there surprised me in that he was very punctual, at least with me. "Well, *c'est la vie!*", I said. Scott had mentioned there was a good chance for an assignment in Dubai.

"The pay is good", he said. "I'll take some pics and write an article about a new hotel, or something like that." I asked him if being in an Arab country was safe for an American. He assured me it was. And, anyway, he explained, "remember, I have friends there." Mentioning this to Margaux, it didn't surprise her.

While waiting for him, she revealed that once in a while he did disappear for a few weeks without an explanation. Joking, I brought up the idea, "Perhaps he's an operative, he might be working undercover. Didn't you meet him at the embassy?" I love spy movies.

"Well", she said tapping her fingers on the table, "I suspected there was something odd about his many trips. He is not selling anything. Such a nice young man, it will be terrible if something were to happen to him".

I've always been an incredulous person. So now, retracing his past movements at Fontainebleau, the private meeting with his friend Daniel—if that was his real name—and the papers he was supposed to have taken with him to Barbizon, made me even more skeptical about his work. We both became silent for a moment, reassessing the possibilities of that idea, but it was getting late. We finally got up and, grabbing our bags—Margaux's a Channel original, mine a very Key West flowery type representing the tropics—left for the bistro.

Le Bon Bock. As Scott had suggested, we were going to Le Bon Bock,[25] which is on the southern edge of the Montmartre district. Half an hour later and a few minutes after two o'clock, there we were.

Compared to other locations in Paris, like the Moulin de la Galette, whose venue became even a TV studio, Le Bon Bock has always been a restaurant at the same location, 2 Rue Dancourt, since 1879—it claims to be the oldest in Montmartre. Usually not visited by tourists, it was the place where, more than one hundred years ago, you could find Toulouse-Lautrec or Picasso or perhaps Guillaume Apollinaire[26] sharing a bottle of Absinthe. The owners have kept the original look of the restaurant, and, once inside, you are transported to the late 1890s with old clocks, tables, chairs and soot-covered paintings. A must for art and history buffs like myself, it reminded me of the pics I'd seen of Barcelona's Los Caracoles.[27]

Margaux and I dressed tastefully for the occasion and I felt like a princess. There we were among the diners, wishing for Picasso to reappear even if he drew my nose coming out of my ear and my unidentified eyes placed vertically.

Because the tables are placed close together and on that day the temperature was pleasant, I didn't feel claustrophobic. When the waiter brought the menu we looked it over and decided it would be a good idea to share a beef *bourguignon*, and Margaux ordered buttered noodles. The bread was perfect, as it usually is in French restaurants. She accompanied the meal with a bottle of Petit Chablis. For dessert, we ordered pistachio creme brulee and a fruit tart. All dishes were cooked according to what was available at the market each day and to the chef's inspiration. Seeing that the chef, especially in France, was the king of the castle, what we ordered was an excellent choice.

The food had been delicious. After dessert, being my friend passionate about after-dinner wines, we enjoyed a French Sauternes. Utilized to close the palate, Margaux, who was an expert in the field, explained in a rather humorous way, "this kind of beverage provides an ambrosial ending to the meal we just savored." We were getting along fabulously.

Retracing my steps. After lunch, I wanted to go back to Sacre Coeur. So we wandered up the hill and relished, while climbing, the most beautiful view of the church. Margaux said she hadn't been to the Basilica in years.

We walked a few blocks to meet with Jules, Margaux's old friend who lived close by and accompanied us to the church with a friend. He was charming and good-looking, perhaps in his 50s, with a bit of an over protracted nose. Jules was an architect whose specialties were churches and their art. He loved to teach all about their architecture and was pleased at being invited to come along. It was a beautiful sight to enjoy as we ascended the hill. He explained the construction of this church had a political bent.[28] Officially, this graceful building was named Basilica of the Sacred Heart of Jesus of Paris, in 1872, by Joseph-Hippolyte Guibert, then the French Archbishop of Paris and Cardinal, in honor of George Darboy, a former Archbishop of Paris, who the *communards* — the uprising of the Paris Commune of 1870-71 — executed, thus becoming a martyr for the resurgent Catholic Church. It is said his successor, Archbishop Guibert, upon climbing the Butte Montmartre in October 1872, was reported to have had a vision. He blurted: "It is here, it is here where the martyrs are. It is here where the Sacred Heart must reign so that it can beckon all to come". The *Assemblee Nationale* (under the French Third Republic) voted in 1873 for its construction, specifying that it was being built to "expiate the crimes of the *communard*", although hostages had been executed on both sides.

Visiting this sanctuary is one of the most important trips anyone could take. This magnificent structure, as I previously said, can be found at the Butte Montmartre, one of the higher hills around the city. To spend time inside is like being in a museum. The walls are covered with incredible pieces of art, paintings and statues. A mosaic in the apse, *Christ in Majesty*, is among the largest in the world. And there you can also admire a Savoyarde bell weighing nineteen tons, outstanding painted ceilings, and an impressive pipe organ. Much more than a religious experience, besides the artwork, the complex also includes a garden with a fountain for meditation. We climbed to the top of the dome to see a spectacular panoramic view of the city, while Jules and his friend sat on a bench talking. Looking down on Paris from the top of Sacred Heart, Margaux shared how disappointed she was that Scott was not there to enjoy it with us. Such a nice guy and now a good friend. Seeing that Scott had vanished, I thought it would be a good time to say a prayer for him and light a candle. Marla was also nowhere to be found and we wondered if she was with him.

After finishing our visit to the basilica, where I had photographed the whole world in the pinkest hues anyone had ever seen, Jules asked us to his home for coffee and honey madeleine cookies baked by him. A perfect ending to a far-reaching afternoon. At about sunset, we went back to Margaux's home.

Back at her place, Margaux got a call inviting her to join a gathering at the Ministry of the Overseas. Never the idler, I then left for Shakespeare and Company where, as it is always the case, a presentation was running. There I met Paloma,[29] from Spain, who, like my cousin Gloria, was studying French at the Soborne. Friendly like me, we talked for a long while.

A few days later Marla showed up and, once again, said she was going to stay in France a while longer. Recounting how she invited herself to tag along with Scott to Amsterdam — a one-day trip — as he held to a thin valise the whole journey, she uttered he was kind and courteous, dropped her off at the Van Gogh Museum and didn't see him again until the trip back. "Weird", she said. On my previous advice, she took the opportunity to learn about Dutch painters, especially Van Gogh. Just by analyzing his output and learning about the artist's life and his health problems, would make anyone who enjoyed art understand how difficult it was and still is to follow that line of work. All of it made us admire the artist even more.

In the meantime, I still had a few days left in France and decided to call Paloma. Inviting her to come along to visit the Rodin Museum; she was thrilled.

Auguste Rodin (1840-1917). The vast work of this genius is at 77 rue de Varenne in a petit palace called Hotel Biron, built for financier Peyrend de Moras, who died in 1732. De Moras loved greenery and had a French classical garden designed for the grounds. After he died the house was rented by his widow to a series of tenants. Later, in 1753, she sold the estate to the duc de Biron— Marshal of France and hero of the Seven Years' War— who added to the grounds an English-style garden. But once Biron died in 1788, it was taken over by different owners and tenants. Nevertheless, the mansion is still known to this day as the Hotel Biron. In the early 20th Century, the property was put up for sale again. Meanwhile, starting in 1905, the writer Cocteau, the painter Matisse, the dancer Isadora Duncan, and Clara, the wife of Rainer M. Rilke, were tenants on the property. Clara was the one who told Rodin about the mansion. Throughout the years the residence has gained a riveting history.

By 1908 the sculptor rented a few rooms on the ground floor and turned them into his studio, and used the garden, which had grown with wild weeds by now, to place there some of his sculptures. In 1911 he took over the entire building, and because by now his reputation was entrenched, the French Third Republic bought the mansion, removed the remaining tenants, and gave Rodin control over the building. In exchange, he gave a considerable amount of his output to the state and lived there till the end of his life. At which time the government transformed the mansion and its garden into the Rodin Museum, where his works would be exhibited and still are. The peaceful garden is one of the most beautiful in Paris. Not only is Rodin's work found there, but we were also able, likewise, to delight in those of his student, the brilliant sculptor and once lover, Camille Claudel (1864-1943). She deserves a place in the garden, as well.

After we finished with Rodin and Claudel, our starving selves crossed the street and bought sandwiches and drinks at a *chartuchery*. We then went back and sat in the garden to appreciate its beauty and talk about the sad ending of Camille's life.

Her troubled existence was documented by her great-niece, Reine-Marie Paris. Two films[30] were produced inspired by the book. Both tell the story of her confinement for life by her brother, Paul (1868–1955), a Christian mystic poet. According to Reine-Marie, in her family "the subject was taboo because bringing it up could reignite the old argument about her internment in a psychiatric asylum, which was considered abusive." There she never sculpted again.

Although she passed away in 1943, her life as an artist was finished when she was confined from 1913 till she died.

After enjoying the experience of knowing Rodin and Camille had probably walked hand in hand through those very gardens, while getting back to Margaux's place I realized my days in France were coming to an end. With my trip almost over, it was my wish to conclude it the way it began, meeting with Scott, if only for an *au revoir*. It had been a magnificent trip, much more than what I'd expected. Having met Scott and Margaux, bumped into Marla, and to have made friends with French, Italians, Spanish, Portuguese, and many other newcomers, with whom I'm still in contact, was an added blessing. All of it made my experience even more superb and unforgetta-

The author at the Grand Trianon

Marie-Antoinette and her children

The Temple of Love

The Petit Trianon

The author at the Hamlet

Pierre Bonnard's *Self-Portrai*

Marie-Antoinette's Hamlet and lake

The author and her bridegroom at Monet's garden in Giverny

The author at the bridge in Giverny

Musée des Impressionnismes Giverny

Museum A. G. Poulain (Vernon)

Maurice Denis' *Self-portrait*

Monet's *Nympheas*

Mary Fairchild's *Self-portrait*

Vuillard's *Coin de Parc*

Anaïs' house at Louveciennes

Monet's House by Blanche Hoschedé,
Monet's stepdaughter

123

Sainte-Chapelle's interiors

Musée de Cluny

Lady and the Unicorn

Monet's *Effet de soleil couchant à Pourville*

124

Butler's *Sunset in Veules-les-Roses*

Franzoni's *A Nursing Goat and Kid*

Monet's *Woman with a Parasol*
(Suzanne Hoschedé)

Monet's house at Giverny

125

The author and Valery in Giverny

MacMonnies' *Tamed Horses*

Bonnard's *Femme au Tub debout*

DiPalma-Falco's *Pair of Cats*

126

ble, including my art classes; they were first-rate. The exposure to mastery and creativity in museums was priceless.

Eventually, Scott showed up and offered to take me to the airport, and Margaux came along. We all promised we would get together again soon.

On my way home via Spain. My mother had arranged for me to visit our relatives in the old country. Summer was kicking off and the temperature was delightful in Barcelona. My aunt's niece-in-law was getting married to a French fellow and I was invited. Elated to see me, Hortensia was also present; we had lots to share. It was a lovely wedding; nothing fancy in a little church outside the city. It was a sunny day and everywhere there were flowers in the fields. The reception took place at a *casa pairal*, an ancestral country house, and afterward we all went back to the city.

While in Barcelona I visited the Picasso Museum. My aunt, who also loves Picasso, wanted to come along. Being there helped me fathom his genius. Picasso's late teens in Barcelona were prodigious. They complemented the first experiences I had been previously exposed to at the Museum of Fine Arts in Boston. Staying for a while with my aunt and her husband, we all had an awesome time together.

Those colorful days of summer. Finally the trip was over and I was on my way home. Once again with friends and family, I shared all about my experiences and the many photographs I had taken. I told my sweetheart I wanted to return to Paris after we got married. He thought it was a perfect idea; however, we would have to save up a lot before leaping across the ocean. In the interim, we spent the summer with friends.

A few days after I arrived, I called my teacher and made an appointment to show her the photographs. She was impressed and pleased with my commitment. I set the day to show the best photographs of my petit assignment, along with other students' work. Once I saw the work on the gallery wall and the honest praise of my fellow students, I knew I had to go back to reprise the experience in a *voyage pour deux*. Mine was meant to be a lasting art project.

Les rêves deviennent réalité. Yes, dreams can become reality. It didn't take me but a couple of years to get back to that magnificent place Paris is. A wedding gift with Jeron, my spirited hubby now by my side, then, more friends were made and more photos were taken. We stayed at the same hotel, the old Sevigne in rue Mahler — still a favorite of mine. Even the clerk at the front desk remembered me.

After touring the city, we made a few outings beyond Paris. Margaux was away in Spain with friends and Scott had pulled a disappearing act like always, so we couldn't meet with him, either. I had previously made plans with Valeria, my friend from Barcelona, who decided she would meet us in Paris. She arrived with her new boyfriend, Ivan. We were planning to travel to the Versailles Palace complex and then to Giverny — neither of us had visited that amazing village made famous by Monet. Valeria was staying at a friend's apartment. Because we would be doing a bit of sightseeing outside Paris, she thought it would be a good idea to rent a car.

Grand Trianon. At sunup, they came for us, and away we went. Years back, when I visited the palace with Margaux, we didn't have time to stop by the Trianons. This time I talked Valeria, who had already seen the palace, into visiting both: The Grand Trianon and Marie-Antoinette's Petit Trianon.

The grounds at Versailles are so extensive—considered the "world's largest royal domain" at a shade above three square miles—we decided to rent bikes. The visit became a grand adventure. We peddled and roamed around the place for several hours. First, we visited the Grand Trianon.

Built by Jules Hardouin Mansart and finished in 1688 on the site of the fragile Porcelain Trianon—this earthenware was a favorite material of Louis XIV,[31] but it deteriorates under the elements—it was demolished and replaced by marble, which is a rock. Constructed for the Sun King and his mistress, Madame de Montespan, who later became his secret wife, the edification is fit for a queen. The king's idea was to escape the formality of court life. It's a single-story palace, elegant and cozy at the same time. The porcelain tiles were replaced by red-pinkish marble from Languedoc and it's still the same as we see it today. Presently it serves as a presidential residence and it is also used to host foreign dignitaries. It has a beautiful courtyard and geometrical French gardens.

Petit Trianon. From the Grand Trianon, still on the grounds at Versailles, we went to the Petit Trianon nearby. It was built in 1758 for Louis XV's mistress, Madame de Pompadour (1721-1764), who was the most influential and dominant lady in the French Court. But Pompadour died of tuberculosis before she could enjoy it. It was later, when Louis XVI ascended the throne in 1775, that he gave the little palace as a gift to Marie Antoinette. Built on the Greek style with classical art elements, inside the structure you'll find elegant woodwork decor; however, the Rococo style developed during King Louis XV's reign, featuring shell-like and scroll motifs, was no longer used. Also, the grounds lost their symmetrical shapes of the typical French garden. They were redesigned by Richard Mique as English-inspired patches, which included lovely rambling paths, hills, streams and a neoclassical Temple of Love.

It was Marie Antoinette who invited the King, but only when she wished, to attend her theater at this Petit Trianon, and to dine with her friends. What was important for the Queen was the privacy she wanted and demanded. In other words, she had her own house devoted to amusements, most of the time.

Falling in love with both Trianons and their gardens, Valeria and I preferred them much more than the enormous palace of Versailles, which included, besides living quarters, also offices for governmental departments. These learning adventures were unmatched.

Although we had made plans to move on and visit Giverny, there was another place that piqued our attention at the Versailles compound.

The Hamlet. Marie Antoinette's delightful retreat was beautiful. Built in 1783, it is a complex of houses based on a romantic dream. Besides her gorgeous Petit Trianon, it was also where the young Queen went to get away from the active and rowdy life at Court. Constructed to bear a similarity to a Norman village, there are eleven buildings around a pond, with stairs and balconies adorned with a variety of flower pots. Each house had its little garden filled with flowers and vegetables. They also planted apple, chestnut and cherry trees. The dreamy structures were used by the Queen, her friends and visitors. The walls were covered with climbing plants, and play swings hung from rafters where the royal children and their friends played. Also, a tower with a beacon by the lake was set, where boat rides and outings were launched. It was a perfect setting for the royals. One of the houses was used as a kitchen. There, dishes were prepared for the gatherings given at the Petit Trianon or the

Hamlet. Actually, the premises had the makings of a working farm, which included livestock. More than a game, it supplied the kitchens of the palaces.

Hungry after so much walking and riding, we went back to the tea room at Versailles to enjoy a snack. This time we ordered the truffle ravioli, accompanied by a chilled rosé; it was delicious and we savored each bite. For dessert chocolate and mint macaroons. It was the perfect ending to our lovely visit. With cravings satiated, a full tank of gas, and already late, we hit the road.

Giverny here we go... Less than an hour's drive away, and armed with a good map, Ivan, who was also a photographer, planned to take photos at Monet's place. We got along great, and Valeria was funny and terrific company—she still is.

The small town, on the southeastern edge of Normandy, is 40 miles northwest of Paris and it had been a dream of mine to visit it from the moment I got to value the work of Monet while visiting the Museum of Fine Arts in Boston. Admiring his paintings where he painted them was unique, and his garden was part of my pursuits, inasmuch as gardening is my thing but never have enough time to dedicate myself to it. The drive to Giverny was pleasant, as we encountered many forests along the way.

Nestled in pastoral surroundings, Giverny is a rural village with flowers everywhere. Here people follow a much slower pace than in the capital. Once in the center, we first visited Monet's house and then walked through the garden as we enjoyed the spring light, which is the best time to bring a camera. I felt like a guest of Monet, sensing his presence all around me.

Claude Monet (1840-1926) lived a good life and was fortunate to spend his last forty-three years at Giverny. He put down roots with his family in 1883 and lived in his paradise until his death. Many of his kin are buried there as well.

First, he rented the house, which came with two acres of land. Then, about ten years later, after having earned enough from his work, he bought the property. In the beginning, only the flower garden, called Clos Normand, sprung up in front of the house. Afterward, he divided the land with flowerbeds, fruit trees, ornamental trees, and a central alley, covered with iron arches, spreading across with climbing roses that are still there to enjoy. The garden was given the form he wanted to create his artwork, including of course the colors and design of an impressionist painting. By 1893 he bought another piece of land on the other side of the road.

This new property was crossed by a small brook he widened to dig the pond, later enlarged and designed to resemble a Japanese water garden. It's in this garden where you find the bridge covered with the wisterias prominent in his painting many times. For those who enjoy gardens and ponds, this is paradise incarnate.

There were several reasons why I wanted to go to Giverny. To start, the serenity found is food for the imagination that fuels creativity. But the most important one to me was to learn about his lifestyle, family relationships, and his awareness of continuance by observing what he did. I wanted to understand how someone could have a career doing what the person enjoys and, at the same time, develop a hobby which, in his case, was gardening. Reading about Monet I realized his secret was at not being alone. His extended family was present and he had the benefit of many gardeners helping him in his endeavor; although Monet always controlled the layouts and how it would look, all that help allowed him, of course, the time to dedicate himself to his art.

Because as an optimist sometimes I idealize that maybe someday I would be able to buy a farm outside

Paris, or in Seville by the Guadalquivir — invariably falling in love with places with rambling rivers — the romantic in me always daydreams and hopes to settle in the countryside to write poems and enjoy nature or perhaps pick up for a song one of those towns that are perched on the side of a mountain in Catalunya. I concoct visions about having dozens of acres surrounding me, where nature in its purest form with waterfalls and flowers envelop me. I want my friends to visit and be inspired by the scenery.

After we finished with Monet and his museum, we walked around the small roads. The people in town were nice. Ivan and I could not stop clicking away, while Jerón and Valeria sat at a bench talking and laughing. Because it was getting late, I convinced them to stay one more night, to get up early and, after breakfast, visit the local American museum and then a stopover at Vernon, eight minutes away across the Seine, and call on the Poulain exhibits.

We decided to stay at *La Pluie de Roses* [Rain of roses] on Rue de Monet. And of course, the B&B had a splendid rose garden. I took a shower and lathered up with an aromatic rose soap which the owner said was left in every room.

We first had tea, which they served near the waterfall. The setting was gorgeous. The place is decorated French Provençal and the garden could be seen from the bedroom window. Later, the owners invited us to join them at the terrace with the other guests for a glass of wine, before going out to dinner. Everyone was friendly.

On the advice of the B&B owners, we agreed to walk leisurely to a nice, small restaurant in the vicinity. Promenading, we noticed marvelous old houses and well-kept gardens fenced in by elegant gates like in Colette's novels. We found the restaurant and resolved to sit in the garden under the trees. A fantastic moon accompanied us and the night was cool and perfect. Life is not rosy and gleaming all the time, but on that night it was. Here we were with the boys. We laughed, clicked our wine glasses, talked about Monet and his magnificent gardens, and thanked Mother Earth. We were able to enjoy the flowers, the happy setting at Giverny, and its romantic village. The dinner was delightful. We all ordered duck *a l'orange*. What better place to savor this dish than in France? Braised and roasted to the right taste and texture, I could savor the thyme, marjoram and parsley in the orange sauce. It was out of this world. It was served with cubed parsley potatoes dressed with a wine and cream sauce. We accompanied the dish with Sauvignon blanc, which had a dry and citrusy liveliness, perfect with duck. And for dessert apricot cake embellished with fresh fruits and covered with apricot marmalade, followed by a small tumbler of Sauternes from Bordeaux, a sweet wine.

It's impossible to visit France and not have a glass of wine with dinner. After finishing our meal and thanking the waiter, Valeria exclaimed laughing, *"la vie est douce"*! And I thought, yes indeed, life is sweet!

What more could we ask? Young and in love, we walked back to the hotel slowly, enjoying, once more, the beautiful hamlet and its architecture. As we strolled, Valeria and I sang a jazzy song made famous by Edith Piaf.

> *Non, rien de rien, Non, je ne regrette rien,*[32]
> *Ni le bien qu'on m'a fait, Ni le mal;*
> *tout ca m'est bien egal,*
> *Non, rien de rien, Non, je ne regrette rien,*
> *C'est paye, balaye, oublié Je me fous du passé!*

As the song continues, the lyrics are very positive. Piaf is letting us know she's starting again from zero, regrets nothing, and that the past has been paid.

We laughed exuberantly. If anyone saw us, it would have seemed to them we were two inebriated nuts—we probably were—out on the town. Unencumbered by our behavior, our beaus hung back talking about sports. They seemed to be enjoying the pleasant walk without distractions.

The next day, after an excellent breakfast of farmer's cheese, apple tarts, crispy bread spread with jam, fresh juice and lots of fruits, we went to explore the other museums which they told us were worth visiting. Both were nearby, the American Museum and the Museum A.G. Poulain of Vernon. After I read about them, we couldn't leave the area without taking a look.

Musée d'Art Américain. In 2009, *Musée d'Art Américain* was renamed the *Musée des Impressionnismes* Giverny. It's a small place down the road from Monet's house, just a stroll away. The architecture of the building is modern, interesting outside and simple inside. The edifice itself seems to be the only modern structure in town, although it is designed with a low profile to fit into the hillside. There are several terraced garden areas attached to the museum as well, which we found to be quite interesting in themselves, and wandering through them is free. The visitor can enjoy the display of flowers even before one approaches the front door. The structure inside is nice and relaxing, and we found it very cool after the heat in the gardens. It's a must place to visit, if you go to Giverny; it doesn't take more than two hours to tour it. It's well organized and they bring excellent collections from the most significant impressionists. Downstairs there is a permanent exhibit of Monet and those friends who were influenced by the impressionist movement; it has paintings that have never traveled to other museums. Its focus is on the impressionist genre only, and it has a rotating special exhibit related to that period.

We strolled around the grounds once more after enjoying the exhibits. The gardens are gorgeous and worth paying another visit. They are remarkable for their colorful arrangement; it's easy to recognize as Claude Monet's territory. Ivan noticed the hay-stacked plot on the garden terrace, which ran into the hillside. It serves as a great backdrop for the more formal gardens and the countryside itself. Being an expert in the field, he felt it had to be a tribute to the haystacks painted several times by Monet and seen in many museums around the world. It was probably designed that way intentionally and presented as an interesting subliminal message.

After viewing the exhibition and while the boys were downing a couple of beers, we visited the gift shop, which it's impressive and a treasure trove of books about art, scarves, cards, jewelry, and much more. All are very well chosen and displayed. I bought several scarves for my aunts and Hortensia, then we walked through the gardens once more.

Hungry by now, we decided to eat outside under the pergolas to relish the incredible French countryside and its cuisine. Even the simplest of dishes are delicious. In the restaurant of the museum, everything they serve is very French. We had mint tea over ice and I ordered quiche with a salad of fresh asparagus and carrots. Valeria had a Camembert grilled cheese sandwich with basil leaves on French bread spread with mustard and country butter all over. It couldn't get better. And the guys delighted in country-ham-and-Gruyère sandwiches, also with mustard, and beer they found "aromatic." Nothing missing and I was glad we were sharing this special moment with our Spanish friends.

Musée A. G. Poulain (Vernon). The next museum is interesting for how it was created. Around 1862, the Brecourt family presented two thousand stuffed birds to the city of Vernon. By 1927, Alphonse-Georges Poulain turned over to the city his collections of archeology and fine arts. Later, in 1964, Vernon was given a collection of paintings and prints by Swiss artist Théophile-Alexandre Steinlen. It was at that time decided to turn the former mansion of the Lemoine de Belle-Isle family—an important clan before the French Revolution—into a museum. The institution was named for Poulain, who was an archeologist and artist; he also became its first curator. This is an incredible half-timbered house, situated at the corner of rues du Pont and Carnot. The original house seemed to have been there since 1577. Then, in the 17th century, a stony wing, typical of those of Louis XIV style, was built. The building itself would be interesting to those who love architecture. According to its history, after the Revolution the place was turned into a hotel and then into a police station until 1964 when it was finally converted into a gallery.

As we walked in, we noticed a staircase, whose wall is decorated with historical portraits. Only in the drawing cabinets, we were able to enjoy the original wood panels. Vernon is one of the few museums in France specialized in animal art; the museum owns over 400 works. Besides paintings and drawings, we enjoyed the lovely animal sculptures, like the one called *A Nursing Goat and Kid* by Francesco Franzoni (1734-1818), also *Pair of Cats* by Enrico-Manfredo DiPalma-Falco (1886-1988), which I adored. We were fascinated by the art style that went from realism to abstraction to contemporary art pieces. I think it is a perfect museum for children. It was exciting to see some canvases by Monet we had never seen. This museum is the only one in the area that exhibits them. In this case, the work is one of the few round pieces he painted—of about 250 water lilies he did. Named *Nympheas*, it was painted in his garden in 1908. Monet and his son donated the work. In Vernon we also saw *Effet de*

Soleil couchant à Pourville [the cliffs of Pourville at sunset], painted in 1896 from a hut on the beach. The work, which is part of a six-canvas series, represents the views of the cliffs at Varengeville west of Pourville. It was donated by his son, Michel, to honor his wife's memory.

Among the paintings in the museum, there is also Blanche Monet's *Monet's House*, and the *Pond at Giverny*, among others. Blanche Monet was Monet's stepdaughter and daughter-in-law. In other words, she was the daughter of Monet's second wife by a previous marriage and was married to Monet's son, Jean. Other French painters were represented at the museum as well. There was Pierre Bonnard (1867-1947), a part-time resident who loved to paint in Vernon by the Seine river; he enjoyed a discreet life with his companion Martha. We were pleased to see *Vallée de la Seine à Rolleboise* and *Femme au Tub debout*, a drawing of a study of a bathing woman from around 1920. Also Édouard Vuillard's (1868-1940) *Coin de Parc* and Maurice Denis' (1870-1943) *Prise de Voile*. Denis, with Bonnard and Vuillard, formed the Nabis trio. This was a Postimpressionist avant-garde group of the 1890s who were also interested in literature.

But French artists are not the only ones we saw there. France has always been a magnet for painters as well as for writers and jazz musicians. We found works by Theodore Earl Butler (1861-1936), an American who settled in Giverny around 1888. In 1893 he married Suzanne, another of Monet's stepdaughters and favorite model. After a long illness, Suzanne died in 1899. Marthe Hoschede, Suzanne's sister, helped Butler raise his offsprings, Jimmy and Lily. He then married Marthe in 1900. Butler gifted the museum landscapes and *Sunset in Veules-les-Roses*.

If France has given America lots of inspiration, Americans also returned good deeds. There we stumbled upon the American Mary Fairchild (1858-1946), who was considered the leader of the American colony at Giverny. Her work, *Coin de parc par temps de neige* [Park Corner in Snowy Weather], is outstanding. She lived in Giverny from 1890 to 1920. Her husband was Frederick MacMonnies, who she married in 1880 and divorced in 1909. They used to invite their friends to stay with them in the summer. The couple studied in Paris, and Frederick, who died in 1937, devoted himself to sculpture. His *Tamed Horses* is in the yard of the museum. The Vernon also exhibits work by landscape artists who are not from Giverny.

The sun was still out when we got back to Paris. We were tired but satisfied with such a fabulous trip. They dropped us off at the hotel, and because pleasant weather was forecasted and Jerón and I still had a few days left, we decided to take advantage of every moment.

Bois de Vincennes and Louveciennes. The next morning Jerón decided to go to the Bois de Vincennes, a magnificent park on the southeastern edge of Paris. He wanted to visit the impressive Château de Vincennes, a fortress next to the park. Paris is one of those awesome European cities replete with parks and gardens. Many of them are former royal hunting grounds. They have lakes that provide boating opportunities, strolling paths, cycling, and the very French sport of kissing. This last one to be practiced on a shaded bench away from probing eyes. Being young and in love, we rehearsed it a great deal.

After relishing some drifting and rowing at Lake Daumesnil in the park, and having a lovely lunch on the grass, we took the train to the western suburbs of Paris to look up the picturesque commune of Louveciennes.

Remembering Anaïs. The desire to go to Louveciennes was borne out of the idea to explore the house flaky writer Anaïs Nin (1903-1977) rented before WWII. She stayed there with her husband, Hugo Guiler (1898-1985), until 1935. This is the residence where she had welcomed Henry Miller,[33] the controversial American writer who visited it many times because, according to her, Henry loved her Spanish maid's cooking. In reality, she was an easy mark, and Henry, a starving writer, took advantage of anyone from whom he could get a good meal, and Anaïs was just another dupe. She wrote about her first adulterous adventures with Henry Miller in her now-famous — perhaps fictional — diaries. The place, at 2 bis rue de Montbuisson, is a private residence and was, at the time we visited it, under renovation. We were able to talk to one of the craftsmen working there and convinced him, in our imperfect French, to allow us to walk through the garden. The windows were being replaced and we were able to look inside. The house had not been well kept, but I could see the walls and floors. It reminded me of Anaïs' description of the place, although dilapidated; it wasn't too different from what she depicted in her writings.

The captivating film, *Henry and June* (1990), which was filmed in Paris and Louveciennes, deals with Anaïs' amorous friendship with Henry. At least that was what she recounted in her diaries, although I have never been able to find a single photograph with the two of them together in Paris.

My hubby's Catalá family, the Güells, are related to Anaïs' father, so Jerón was also curious about the house, which is more than two hundred years old. Anaïs' father, Joaquín Nin Sr., was a famous composer and pianist in the first half of the 20th Century; it was more than mere inquisitiveness what drove us to make the trip to Louveciennes. The village is still lovely and looks similar to how it did in Anaïs' time. We were glad we saw the house and I felt the ghosts of yesteryears all around us.

But it was not only Anaïs the one who enjoyed the little town of Louveciennes. Impressionist painters

Monet, Renoir, Cassatt, Sisley, and Pissarro sometimes lived and also painted there in the 1890s. I wouldn't be surprised if Anaïs had decided, in a romantic impulse, to move there from Paris. But also the rent was significantly less, and her husband, Hugo, was also meeting the financial obligations of her mother and brother. We left France behind after Louveciennes and traveled back to Spain by train to visit Jerón's cousins and aunts in Bilbao. There we stayed for a week and finally returned home.

Paris will forever be in my heart. Once we graduated from college, throughout the years, we've always visited Paris on our way to Spain. On one occasion, my globe-trotting friend, Juanita, a widow who forever was looking for new adventures, joined us—born in Cuba, her father was a Spanish native from the northern coastal city of Santander.

My trustworthy friend was fun. She frequently confided how she admired Cayetana, 18th Duchess of Alba, who read poetry and enjoyed travel. Cayetana had expressed her favorite cities were Seville, Paris and Venice. This gave Juanita the idea of visiting all three as the opportunity presented itself. On this trip, it was decided to stay in Paris for a few days. Juanita was thrilled.

Having ancestors from the Rosselló—a northern region shared by Spain and France—Jerón made arrangements and continued on to Catalunya. He had made plans to chase partridges in Llessui with a friend. The hamlet, at 4,650 feet high, is a small village in the Pyrenees mountains about 20 miles from Andorra. It is where his great-grandfather was born and where today skiers enjoy rushing down a pretty scary mountain. In those treacherous curves I also learned to drive stick-shift.

But now we were in Paris and Juanita was excited. Like Johann Wolfgang Goethe said, "Whatever you can do, or dream you can do, begin it. Boldness has genius, power, and magic in it!" She had taken French lessons at the French Alliance in New York, and I, of course, again with my inseparable camera, was as enthusiastic as ever. The idea of taking a few more pics motivated me.

La Maison Fournaise. After giving Juanita the typical tour of Paris, we went on to visit La Maison Fournaise, which had been closed for a long time. We found it by the Seine at Chatou, west of Paris, where Pierre Auguste Renoir (1841-1919) painted, among others, *The Rowers' Lunch* (1875), and *Luncheon of the Boating Party* (1881). This last one is known in French by the name of *Le Déjeuner des canotiers*, and is now at the Phillips Collection in Washington, D.C.

La *maison* was a watering hole for the young impressionist painter, his friends, and models. Regrettably, it was closed in 1906 and abandoned for many decades thereafter. The building fell apart and, luckily, it was restored in 1990. Today the place is, once again, a restaurant located in the now known *Île des Impressionnistes*. Renoir once wrote to a friend: "I can't leave Chatou because my painting is not finished yet. It would be nice of you to come down here and have lunch with me. You won't regret the trip, I assure you. There isn't a lovelier place in all of Paris's surroundings." Accordingly, ever since I saw *Luncheon of the Boating Party*, I had been excited about visiting the restaurant. What a bewitching setting!

We had lunch on the terrace at the same spot Renoir painted his famous work. We both enjoyed a tasty *gratin de saumon au champagne et raisins,* washed down with smooth Chardonnay; for dessert *crème brulée à l'ancienne* as an accompaniment. At that moment I felt life couldn't be better.

There were also some nice-looking couples savoring the moment who, upon seeing my camera, handed me theirs and asked me to record the moment for them. The only one missing was Renoir, but I felt he was there, anyway.

From the balcony, continuing the practice of yesteryear, you could see young men, accompanied by pretty ladies, boating on the Seine. Nothing could be better to catch the flavor of the French. It was truly romantic! The young couple I had just photographed were from Belgium and asked us to share a light drink. What a fabulous day we were having. And this was only the beginning of our adventure!

The sky was almost turquoise and I took advantage of the light by clicking away. Feeling like an impressionist myself, we were reliving those moments when Renoir and friends gathered there to enjoy life as no one else dared to do. You could always take to heart, looking at his paintings, what the French called *joie de vivre*. And that was what I experienced at that moment. I thanked God I was able to visit the place; cheerful and blessed at the same time.

Following the visit to Maison Fournaise, we went to the Latin Quarter in the center of Paris and stopped by the Musée de Cluny. This is a medieval structure built over Roman baths. The edifice is one of the oldest constructions in the city and is supposed to have been a private residence. Its exact origins remain a mystery, albeit some consider it having been commissioned by the *Le Viste*, a noble family of the late 1400s. There we found the tapestry *Lady and the Unicorn* from the late 15th century, among others — Juanita collects figures of this mythical creature.

From Cluny, we continued to Sainte-Chapelle, an arresting chapel with magnificent stained glass windows — you are surrounded by them — near Notre Dame

Cathedral. Built at Louis IX's direction from 1243 to 1248, this holy chapel is a masterpiece of Gothic Rayonnant style. We were in awe of its beauty. It is easy to become overwhelmed with spiritual joy, even if one is not religious. Sitting serenely while looking at them, Juanita turned emotional and shed a tear or two.

La Lucarne aux Chouettes. After that profoundly felt experience at Sainte-Chapelle, we met with Margaux as planned. The two ladies liked each other immediately. Although I had not seen Margaux for a few years, she still looked superb.

Margaux, as energetic as ever, came up with the magnificent idea of visiting Leslie Caron[34] at her bed and breakfast. She often enjoys Leslie's company as she walks her dog near her residence, and was planning to visit her new B&B in Burgundy with a friend, but the friend couldn't make it. So instead she asked us if we wanted to take the short trip to La Lucarne aux Chouettes. Being a widow and very independent, Margaux always had her traveling bag ready and was forever enthusiastic and filled with curiosity about everything.

Soon we were on our way to the inn, The Skylight with Owls — my most accurate translation. I had read in a lady's magazine that Leslie would drop by the small hotel once in a while. Our hope was she would be there to tell her how much we still enjoyed her films, especially *Gigi* and *An American in Paris* — my favorites musicals.

We arrived at Leslie's place in less than two hours. The inn is in Villeneuve-sur-Yonne, 87 miles southeast of Paris. It is surrounded by virtually an intact medieval wall built during the 12th century. A former residence of kings, the town has a long and amusing history.

The first thing we noticed, as we entered the walls of the city, was the magnificent Notre Dame church, which is a mixture of Gothic and Baroque architecture,

Gate of Joigny at Villeneuve-sur-Yonne

Old church at Villeneuve-sur-Yonne

Bridge over Yonne river at Villeneuve-sur-Yonne

Poster for the film "Gigi"

Leslie Caron at La Lucarne aux Chouettes

145

Vincent van Gogh

Above: The "stairs" today that Van Gogh painted
Below: Van Gogh's *Village street and stairs with figures*

Paul Gauguin

Leslie Caron's La Lucarne aux Chouettes

Van Gogh's *Starry Night*

Dr. Gachet

Dr. Gachet's house

Van Gogh's *The Red Vineyard*

Dr. Gachet by Van Gogh

Dr. Gachet's drawing of
Van Gogh in deathbed

147

Van Gogh's *Wheatfield with Crows*

The author and Juanita at Van Gogh's grave

Dr. Gachet's daughter, Marguerite, by Van Gogh

My daughter, Yasmin, at Rambouillet

Van Gogh's *Church at Auvers*

The author at Church of Auvers

Daubigny Museum at Auvers

Colette's house at Aint-Sauveur-en-Puisaye

Camille Pissarro

Van Gogh's
Café Terrace at Night (Arles)

Parisian dog by Yasmin

Van Gogh's famous sunflowers

The author in front of Auberge Ravoux

and the most important building in the small village. Impressed by the beauty of the structure, I asked Margaux, who was now driving, to park the car so we could amble around the town.

Aroused by the beauty of the half-timbered houses, a sightseeing walk took us only about a half-hour to go from one end, at the Gate of Sans, to the other, where the Gate of Joigny stands. At this last exit, a museum dedicated to local history and art is located; we visited it the next day. I took photographs of the Yonne river and the gorgeous 13th-century Gothic bridge, which is the only one connecting both sides of the town over the lazy tributary.

Once you enter this burg, the visitor might forget centuries have gone by as time stops. The place makes you feel, I imagine, the way the original dwellers did. In my desire not to forget the magic and with hardly a tourist in sight, my camera went into high gear as I clicked away relentlessly.

We finally arrived at Ms. Caron's Inn, which is located in a 17th Century, picturesque structure on the right bank of the river. Even with only four guest rooms, the inn was spacious enough for us and the few others who were visiting. It was better than I expected. The atmosphere is comely and the grounds splendid and peaceful. Everyone was very polite and helpful, including the restaurant chef who came out to welcome us. And yes, this one was a lucky day. We had the unbelievable surprise of meeting with Ms. Caron, who was there for the weekend with her cute Shih Tzu by her side. It just happened that a well-known magazine was writing an article about the inn and Leslie was giving an interview. She looked even more beautiful than I remember from her many films; Juanita was struck by her presence.

Although many years have passed since *Gigi*, her beautiful blue eyes, gregarious personality and charm came through. She was warm, polite and accommodating, making us feel at home in her petite inn.

The long trip was worth the effort. Margaux talked to her for a while. I heard them laugh while walking on the terrace. Leslie was happy to meet her once more. They had friends in common.

Margaux later told me they both promised to keep in touch, for, at the moment, Leslie lived close to her in Paris.

That night we had dinner at the inn's restaurant and were pleased by the specialties of the house and their desserts, which were good enough to die for. We ordered the guinea fowl with truffles. Of course, I didn't count calories. After dinner, we walked toward the watercourse to watch how it flowed gracefully to Montereau to join the Seine thirty-five miles away. We weren't alone, though, there were also a few American students sitting by the stream, playing guitar and singing. The whole experience was dreamlike. The temperature was cool as we shared with the students a vigorous bottle of champagne to celebrate the occasion. We sat, laughed and made jokes, telling stories of our trips and our many misadventures together.

We slept pleasantly that night and left early the next morning, after enjoying a cup of very strong coffee, of course. There were still more adventures to experience. Juanita, who was a movie buff, had a fabulous time, too. She got along so well with Margaux, that they invited each other to go on vacations together.

Sometime later I discovered that, unfortunately, Ms. Caron sold the inn and moved to London, where her children and grandchildren live. Nevertheless, I have been told the new owners still run the inn just as magnificently as Ms. Caron did.

Colette again. On this trip, I persuaded my friends to travel to the now open Colette´s Museum. Knowing the town, for I had walked its entire length some years before, now she had her own place and her collection is snuggled into the fertile, colorful countryside in her hometown of St-Sauveur-en-Puisaye. Also, her childhood home can be visited as well.[35]

Both my friends enjoyed Colette's writings and gladly accepted the idea. Juanita had read many of her stories while taking classes at the French Alliance. To her, meeting Leslie Caron and visiting Colette´s town were two of the high points of her trip.

It was Colette's daughter, Colette de Jouvenel, who came up with the idea to create a museum dedicated to her mother. But the unfortunate woman died in 1981 before it became a reality. The idea was not abandoned, however, and her descendants pressed on with it. Because Colette ignored her daughter all of her life, we can say the museum is a true testament to someone willing to forgive.

The place is a shrine. They brought together articles from her estate, especially belongings from her Paris apartment in the Palais-Royal, including furniture. Entering the exhibition, imprinted on the floor you'll be able to learn Collete's addresses where she lived, embodying also her house in the village and her last Parisian home. In addition, we found the names of those who were important to her, consisting of her family, artists friends, and writers. An interesting idea in the designs of the displays is that the titles of her many books are engraved in golden letters on the stairs that go up to the top of the old chateau. On the upper floor, a documentary video in French is shown about her life with comments from her contemporary writers and artists. It gave me the excuse to practice the language—what I didn't understand, Margaux translated for me.

Among the collection, there are cat prints from two of her books. There are pretty glass paperweights and glass cases filled with butterflies — which I particularly love and also collect — along with many personal letters. But I didn't see any missives — unlike with the marquise de Sévigné — from or to her daughter. Colette was prolific, with over fifty novels, in addition to short stories, film reviews and diaries. Despite the fact that she was one of the most famous French writers for many years, by now many experts feel she might not have been the best France had to offer.

Over coffee, we discussed how courageous this young girl from a small village in Burgundy was; how she managed to leave family behind never to return, and move to Paris with her much older husband. Even though Henry Gauthier-Villars also wrote copiously, he never evolved into a well-known author. Considering evidence, he seemed to have been invidious of her talents.

Van Gogh's village. Going back to Paris from Colette's hamlet with time to spare, I asked Margaux if we could circumvent the city and drop by Auvers-sur-Oise, the village where Vincent van Gogh[36] (1853-1890) died and is buried. I'd wanted to visit it for the longest time — only once, I remember, we stopped there for just an hour. Juanita seconded my motion and Margaux happily agreed. Thus, this time I finally sojourned to the pretty little town, which is only thirty miles from Paris.

Comparing it to old photographs I've seen, the aspect of the town is the same as when Van Gogh lived and painted there. We found it to be a real country village, beautiful and quaint, surrounded by functioning farms. Of the many artists I like, Vincent is the one that gives me a true appreciation of what talent means. Perhaps because he was not only gifted but also fragile; he was not unlike the temperament of many writers and artists I've known.

Born in the southern part of the Netherlands next to Belgium, this son of a clergyman tried to become a preacher himself, but it didn't work out. Finally, in his 20s he decided to become an artist; Vincent loved to draw and had failed at everything else. Studying art for a stretch in Belgium, where he discovered Japanese prints, the still-developing painter left for Paris in 1886 to help his brother, Theo, who was the manager of Goupil's art gallery. Vincent was thus exposed to modern art for the first time and it affected his style greatly. In Belgium, the future trailblazer used dark colors, but once in Paris, he dumped them after discovering the impressionist palette. It was then he adopted vibrant shades and hues. Also leaving behind the traditional methods he had used, he also began to channel the tools post-impressionists used.

There is something truly special about his paintings that makes the viewer emotional. Margaux, likewise, loved his paintings. She told me a husband of a friend had bought a small drawing by him some years back and that she later got as a divorce settlement. "You certainly know fascinating people", I said to her. She laughed while nodding her head.

We arrived early with plans to continue on our way to Paris once we saw everything; after all, it's just a hamlet. But upon arriving there, as the sights where he painted began to look more engaging, we realized one more day to enjoy the little town and the museums was in the offing. Consequently, we made a reservation to spend the night at a B&B five miles from Auvers.

For lunch, we went to the venerable and charming 144-year-old, Auberge Ravoux, which has been restored to reflect its historical past. The restaurant has been decorated to evoke the time Van Gogh lived and dined there. The food is traditionally French—slowly cooked meat with tarragon, lavender, thyme, butter...—probably the same fare they served in those days. The building is also known as "Van Gogh's House." Upstairs is where he lived and spent the last days of his very sad life. At the *auberge* or inn, he ate when it was then a simple cafe, with good country food served. At the bar, which is still there and probably looks the same, Vincent used to enjoy absinthe, his favorite drink.

The partially-filled restaurant had a solemn atmosphere. We sat right below the room where he died. Realizing this, and talking about him, was truly a heartfelt and poignant experience. I told Margaux I had the feeling he could walk in at any moment. Yes, the carrot-top painter with a sad countenance, carrying with him his latest painting and knowing markedly well it would not sell. However, we were pleased to be there, so close to his genius. It was an experience like no other.

We wanted to eat something the locals ate and ordered lamb accompanied with a puree of parsnips, a homegrown white wine—Margaux knew her wines—and for dessert a no-one-was-counting-calories chocolate mousse and absinthe ice cream, of course. We finished with a cup of excellent coffee.

The next morning we stopped by the small bookstore at Auberge Ravoux. They offered illustrated books about Van Gogh, and I bought one recounting his times in Arles, in the south of France. I also got a few posters depicting several of his works, and gave charming Juanita *Café Terrace at Night*. She loved Vincent's work also.

It was in Arles (1888) where he painted his now-famous sunflowers. The idea, when he moved to Arles, was to start an artist colony. He was joined by Paul Gauguin, who he met through Theo, Vincent's brother. But the Dutch marvel's mental malady began to show a few days after they settled down, and then the notorious incident of the mutilated ear took place. Right after the event and fearing for his life, Gauguin told Theo, who was his agent, that his relationship with Vincent was over, and left. The artist was deeply troubled and getting worse. Now, alone in Arles, by the end of the year he decided to commit himself to the nearby asylum in Saint-Remy-de-Provence. He remained there for more than a year. While at the sanatorium, he kept painting and created one of his most popular works, *Starry Night*.[37] Yet, during his lifetime, he only sold one painting, *The Red Vineyard*. It was sold in Brussels for about $80 a few months before he died. It is now at the National Pushkin Museum in Moscow.

When Theo — who believed fervently in his talent and supported him financially — felt his brother had recovered from his mental breakdown, he encouraged him, at the end of the 1880s, to move to Auvers — in the north of Paris. Vincent stayed at the *auberge* for a few weeks through May to July 1890.

There, Theo asked Dr. Paul Gachet (1828-1909), who was recommended by another painter, Camille Pissarro (1830-1903), to look after Vincent. This physician used homeopathic medicine and specialized in nervous disorders. For a while, the good doctor was able to help him. In this peaceful village, he was very productive. In Auvers, inspired by the gentle landscape and the nature of its residents, according to Gachet, Vincent seemed to be at peace working every day. He painted the doctor's portrait several times, and that of his daughter, Marguerite, playing the piano; he also painted his isolated room in the inn.

After looking through the books, we visited Vincent's room, which is very small, and later watched an interesting slide show about his life. Being there, closer to this praiseworthy painter with a sensitive soul, was inspiring, and my friends agreed. It was a sign of respect that his windowless room, above the *Auberge Ravoux*, was never rented after he died. The French love art and respect their painters; this can be seen by the way they bring it out in the open.

It is easy to see the village is a shrine to him. There are panels of the artist's work all around town, giving the visitor an idea of what sites he painted there. Just strolling through the village is a learning experience. Walking the same roads he used to roam through made us excited and sad at the same time. For a moment I again had the strange feeling he was right there with us. It is terrible to think of how many creative people had difficult, emotional lives. I have befriended a few. Artist and writer Roberto Yanes, who I admired, ended his life the same way Vincent did.

But Van Gogh was not the only artist who settled in Auvers. Before him, in 1861, Charles Daubigny (1817-1878), a precursor to impressionism, also lived there. In the village we found Daubigny's museum, and also his studio-house. Some of the rooms look out to a pretty garden filled with flowers. Van Gogh painted these gardens several times and the work can be seen in Amsterdam.

Besides the work by Daubigny, in this stunning house, we were inspired by Jean Corot's (1796-1875) paintings, the landscape and portrait artist who always came around to visit. Also, Honoré Daumier's (1808-1879) work is there, and others who were Daubigny's friends. Paul Cézanne loved Auvers, and so did Pissarro. With his Barbizon friends, Daubigny worked in this peaceful town nestled by the Oise river.

Once we study Corot's work, we realized he foresaw the *plein-air* style of Impressionism. However, his palette was more restrained, less colorful, and his landscapes were painted more traditionally. I still like the impressionist use of luminous colors better.

The artists who came to Auvers were motivated by the light and the reflection of the clouds on the river's surface, and in winter they were inspired by the soft snow covering its frozen expanse.

A look back at paintings by Vincent appeared as contrived in a whim. Like the one called *The Rain*, showing the fields and distant houses near the asylum at Saint-Remy while raining, also *The Church at Auvers*, which he painted from the rear; a strange alternative since most painters would choose to depict the front of the building. But Vincent's personality had no equal and his choices showed it. He kept working fiercely every day, conceiving seventy-seven paintings and dozens of sketches in Auvers alone. Many of them have now sold for millions.

We went on and visited Dr. Gachet's house. Toward the end of Van Gogh's life, the physician kept track of Vincent in the last place he lived. Gachet's *maison* was a swift walk from the inn and, to our surprise, the building, which is now a museum, is on a hill with a fantastic view of the valley, town and the Oise river. The garden is multi-level, and he collected the leaves for his homeopathic treatments from this colorful retreat. Gachet also invited Pissarro, Cézanne and other painters from the Barbizon school group to accompany him and his family on picnics.

Although Vincent was not the only artist who lived and worked in Auvers, Van Gogh's work is unique. Vincent had written Theo from Auvers that he felt he was a failure and that his life was a waste. Then, on 27 July, at age thirty-seven, he stumbled back into his room from a wheat field where he had shot himself in the chest, dying two days later. The charitable Dr. Gachet, who was an amateur artist, did an etching in black on laid paper of Van Gogh on his deathbed. The red-haired wonder could have been painting crows in the field when he shot himself. The stormy and turbulent masterpiece, *Wheatfield with Crows*,[38] is believed to be his last work. At his funeral, Dr. Gachet eulogized him, "He was an honest man...and a great artist. He had only two goals, humanity and art." Although some experts might not agree, after examining this painting several times at the Van Gogh Museum in Amsterdam, I believe it certainly feels like a suicide message to the world from this troubled painter. During his lifetime he was never recognized; ironically, he became a legend and his legacy are his paintings.

As the day drew to a close, we walked all over the picturesque town. It was a cool and pleasant night. Leisurely we strolled along and stopped at a charming place missed before and had a light dinner. Everything was delicious. We talked for a while with some visiting Americans, giving them some tips before turning in.

The next morning, the three of us visited the 13th Century church at Auvers. Later we continued walking through green fields to the cemetery. The very same fields van Gogh painted so many times while there. At Chemin des Vallees we found not only Vincent's grave, who was buried the day after he died, but also that of Theo, his brother. Although he died six months later, it took his widow, Johanna, thirty years to move his remains from Holland to Auvers to rest by Vincent's side. No one knows why it took her that long or even why she did it.

Going back to Paris we took our time, taking little detours and stopping along the way to enjoy the scenery. It had been an unforgettable trip with Juanita, and Margaux was, as always, marvelous company.

Back at Margaux's apartment, we stayed one night before continuing to Barcelona, where my whole family was waiting. In Barcelona we had a baptism to attend and, after the celebrations, Juanita returned home.

After his shooting exploits, I found Jerón waiting in the wine region of Vilafranca del Penedès, to the south of Barcelona, and there we made plans to travel by car using the coastal route, stopping at Valencia, Alicante,

Malaga and Seville. In Seville, we visited old friends once more. Then headed for Madrid to take in the sights and share some time with Jerón's cousins. But I'll leave that adventure for another book, because, to be fair, Madrid also deserves a meaningful reflection.

April in Paris. Soon it will be spring in Paris, and, while working on the photographs for the Alliance Francaise, I kept reminiscing about that fabulous first trip with my godmother, Hortensia, to the city of my dreams. An educational journey then, I didn't realize my falling in love with that magic city would become a recurrent getaway as we were on our way to visit family and friends in Spain.

As the years went by. On my penultimate trip, because there will always be another, I enjoyed the streets of Paris as a family, with Jerón and our daughter, Yasmin. We walked by the Seine again with the latest equipment in tow. My idea was well thought out. Enjoying certain maturity and seemingly wiser now with a digital camera, the idea was to capture it the way I once envisioned it.

Decades ago as a student, and under the advice of *mon bon ami*, Scott, capturing Paris in all her potential and glorious colors was the goal. Having the same aim now, but focusing on using new techniques was as crucial as my mission. I had to learn to use a new camera, computers and programs. If in my college days the exhibit held only a few photographs, now the concept was to share my experience of these journeys with a wider audience and new images.

Sous le ciel de Paris. I can definitively say there is a different Paris in each one of us beneath the Parisian sky. I've convincingly told my friends that you don't need an eternity to savor the pleasures of that lovely metropolis. All that is required is to have body and soul intertwined and ready for this outstanding experience. And, if by chance, while there, someone comes along and wakes up emotions you had forgotten, don't analyze the moment, simply enjoy it. Because just like the land we once dreamed about but had never seen, with this adventure you will find your inner self most refreshingly. It's the self you didn't know was there.

Paris doesn't break hearts, she mends them. There is always something new to discover at every corner. This magical place is like a bottomless treasure chest, bringing us forever a new surprise.

Today, far away in my Caribbean retreat, sitting on my balcony and looking at my growing, flowering garden, it's comforting to look back and remember that on the other side of the ocean there is France, a marvelous stretch of land replete with beauty, wonder, and rich history in its metropolis as well as in the countryside. And of course, it's delightful to recall the many friends I made there.

After my exhibit, we decided the next venture to Europe will take us across the Atlantic Ocean by ship. I was inspired after watching old newsreels of Grace Kelly arriving in Monaco for her wedding with Prince Rainier. We want to feel the impact of that land while getting closer to the shore. Then, we'll continue our journey and visit charming and romantic villages in search of *La France profonde*.

J'ai adoré chaque instant. Yes, I cherished every moment. It took me almost a year to fashion my 21st Century Paris exhibit. Choosing the right photograph brought back memories of my good friends and the fun we once had while coming upon and discovering all those out-of-the-way, magic places.

Indeed, we are no longer the innocent, young kids we once were. But on that first trip by myself, and others that followed, although the homeless and destitute can also be found there—like Scott used to say—especially nowadays, I concentrated on the mellow side of the city. The images that make us dream of rainbows and pots of gold. Life is too short not to do so.

Unfortunately, *mon cher ami* Scott had disappeared the same way he once materialized: Suddenly like a gentle breeze; not knowing if I would ever see him again.

When it was finally time for my one-woman show to take place, I sent an invitation to Margaux and another one to Scott in her care—his location was always a riddle.

Like my godmother Hortensia once did, Margaux and Scott made Paris more accessible and a most bewitching place. They allowed me to enjoy the city and its neighboring towns the way only a native could. These new friends had been fun and affectionate. And I got the feeling, as time went by, they were angels who appeared in my path to help make my adventures a success, even more so than anyone could ever envisioned. They had been the perfect companions to enhance my journey.

Margaux sent her regrets and acknowledged she had passed my invitation to Scott before he took off for a "new assignment." He was as enigmatic about his whereabouts as ever. According to her, Scott kept on traveling to faraway countries, but never displayed his photographs. In her case, she had a wedding to attend in Spain—her friend was getting married for the fifth time.

Ever the adventurer. By happy chance, my dear Marla made the trip. She had stayed in Paris after I left and always kept in touch. In the meantime, she had been married several times. The last beau is one of those princes without a crown who abound throughout Europe.

Disappointed Scott and Margaux would not be there with me, for they had been such memorable friends, to my surprise, on the day of the exhibit a perfumed, rose-colored envelope with a card was delivered to my home. It had the Alexandre III bridge on the front. A metaphor perhaps? It just said: At last. Devotedly, Scott.

J'adore Paris. Life experiences have taught me to savor the moment and I've always been able to do so. As Joseph Campbell used to say: "You have to follow your bliss". It's true that Paris is no longer the fiery femme fatale of Hemingway's days. It is now a matron of sedate charm, replete with immigrants of all types. Nonetheless, one of these springs I'll be back to bask in her beauty once more because, like an illusionist, I have the ability to make of her whatever I want it to be.

No doubt Paris is always a good subject. In line with what Rick said to Ilsa in the film *Casablanca*: "We'll always have Paris." I knew that was also true for me. Ah, yes!, "Paris is worth a mass."[39] But I feel she deserves even more.

Ce n'est jamais la fin

Finally, many years after my first trip, the Paris display at the French Alliance took place. On that day, the local newspapers sent their photographers and many other publications announced the exhibit: *Paris: Poetic Images of Night and Dawn*. It was a special moment and I was thrilled to be alive and young enough to enjoy it.

Having had difficult and determining moments in my life, on that day I was fortunate to experience the opposite: Sitting on a cloud, living a dream. One of those times impossible to recreate. On a professional level, it was as joyful as when I published *Sugar Cane Blues*, my first book of poetry, years ago.

From the thousands of pictures taken in France throughout the years, I selected thirty to present to art lovers. There was no room for more.

It was a special evening. It turned out to be an unforgettable moment in my life. With all that joy around me, I didn't want it to end. Many of my friends were in attendance to cheer me on and to applaud my efforts. On that night the French Alliance was filled to capacity, and even the Director, Monsieur Timon, was surprised by the number of people who wished to celebrate that special night with me. I was truly overwhelmed by the love and camaraderie they demonstrated. Danielle Ferré-Culas, the delightful Associate Director at the Alliance, who welcomed my idea from the get-go, was also there.

My good friend, Emilio Guerra, college professor and expert sommelier, had generously offered to provide the French wine and help decant it till the night was over. We also offered cheeses of all kinds, French bread, sausages and desserts. Everyone was delighted, while listening to romantic French songs by Edith Piaf and Yves Montand.

Among many others, there were professors, poets, writers, artists, dancers, media personalities, physicians, political activists, and everyone from the Alliance, who were helpful and nice enough to also drop by.

Of the friends that come to mind, there was Silvia Serrú, a wonderful Cuban lady whose grandfather was French. She was thrilled to help me organize the exhibit. There was Georges Ceada, a French-Spaniard and former navy man, who taught French and guided me in how to price the work. Also Julio Matas and Luis Gonzalez Cruz, both excellent writers and academics, surprised me with their enthusiastic presence; Cuban-born Andre Avellanet, passionate poet and writer, whose family is from Catalunya; trusted friend Juan Cueto-Roig, a contemporary poet, raconteur and man of class, who was always traveling throughout Europe, was not able to make it, but, to my delight, sent a gorgeous basket of fresh flowers of all types and colors; writer Zilia Laje, who dashed to the exhibit after the presentation of her latest book; professors and writers Ellen Leeder and Ofelia Hudson, ladies who forever encouraged me to do what gave me joy; poet and artist Mireya Urquidi, from Palm Beach and Bolivia; María Antonia Díaz de Valenzuela, a fine educator who was kind enough to show up even after a busy day at work.

The greater they are, the humbler they act. The renowned Cuban Sculptor Tony López came to see my work and was there until the end; modernist painter, Miguel Nin, who is also a distant cousin of Anaïs Nin, was present; the distinguished Cuban Museum director, Ofelia Tavares, surprised me with her presence; and with her, partaking in the pleasant evening, was museum board member and accountant Félix Pérez; to my wonderment, Luis David and Nenita, editors of the society column of *Diario Las Américas*, dropped by with their photographer, to enjoy the presentation, and also Norma Niurka, a pleasant critic from the *Miami Herald*, was there.

Let's not forget Frank Fernández, a philosophical anarchist, author and friend, who, as editor of *Guángara Libertaria*, always made me laugh. It was also a pleasant surprise to see Miguel Saavedra there, the leader of the Cuban political group, *Vigilia Mambisa,* in Miami; architect Ignacio Carrera-Justiz i Bacardí; Univisión executive, Raúl Toraño.

Hortensita Coalla, proud daughter of Cuban diva Hortensia Coalla Raveiro came to see my work. And so did the *parisienne*, Simone VanDyck with her partner Rogelio Rodríguez, professional dancers. Long ago, after leaving Cuba, Simone and Rogelio made their home in Paris and choreographed at the Moulin Rouge.

Because the exhibit lasted a month, other notables were able to visit in the following weeks. Among them, the wonderful pianist Olga Díaz; Peruvian friend, Aldo Tassi, a world traveler and cyclist; Spanish friend from Asturias, Cristina Llerandi, owner of the chain *Delicias de España*; poet Sara Martínez-Castro; author Ileana García Monserrat. Last but not least, Cuban theater director, Julio Pedro Gómez, was at the reception and returned the following week with friends.

It has been a while. I know there were many more in attendance that I've missed mentioning; my most sincere apology to them. However, I just want to extend that I'm glad you were there with me.

NOTES

1. Born Édith Giovanna Gassion, she got the moniker, Piaf, a vernacular for sparrow, later on.

2. After a four-year renovation that ended recently, it is well worth visiting.

3. Baron Haussmann (1809-1891), of German extraction, excelled as a public official before his appointment to lead the renewal of Paris. Selected for his energy and cleverness and hated for his arrogance, he nevertheless left his imprint on the City of Light to this day.

4. Emperor Napoleon III (1808-1873), first president of France during the Second Republic (1848-1852), turned dictator and ruled as an emperor till 1870 when he fell prisoner to the Germans after losing at the Battle of Sedan. Eventually he went into exile and died in England, where he is buried.

5. José Maria Sert (1874-1945), one of the most outstanding muralist of his time, focused on large-scale work of walls and ceilings. Besides cathedrals and churches, he also painted murals at the Waldorf-Astoria in NYC, 30 Rockefeller Center, also in NYC, the League of Nations in Geneva, and the chapel at Liria Palace in Madrid.

6. Considered by many a pivotal point in the history of Western civilization similar to the Fall of Rome, the causes that ushered it had roots in both the Seven Years' War and the American Revolution. It triggered the decline of the absolute monarchies and the arrival of modern republics and democracies that eventually saw the rise of nationalism.

7. The Paris Commune of 1871—not to be confused by the Paris Commune that formed during the French Revolution (1789-1795)—was a short-lived uprising where Parisian radicals blocked streets and fought the French Army after the debacle and disarray that followed the Battle of Sedan and the imprisonment of Napoleon III. The Commune itself influenced Karl Marx's ideas greatly.

8. Sévigné, Marie de Rabutin-Chantal, The letters of Madame Sévigné to her daughter and friends.

9. Letter from Bussy-Rebutin to madame de Seneville, 28 April 1678.

10. Beginning in the 17th Century, the leaders of France have been known to engage in copious extramarital affairs. For example, Louis XIV had fourteen mistresses, Louis XV also fourteen—except that Louis XVI had none—Napoleon had a few, and in recent times, except for Charles de Gaulle's disciplined personal life, Mitterrand, Giscard, Chirac, Sarkozy and Hollande all had liaisons. On the personal life of Giscard d'Estaing, for instance, Le Monde reported that he used to leave a sealed letter stating his whereabouts in case of an emer-

gency. In their 2006 bestseller, *Sexus Politicus*, two authors expose how in France sex, love and politics are inseparable.

11. Most recently, in 2019, the wedding of Jean-Christophe Napoleon Bonaparte, a descendant of the emperor's youngest brother, Jerome.

12. The story of the heirs to the Principality of Monaco in the early part of the 20th Century is captivating, full of twists and intertwined with life in the district of Montmartre in Paris. Prince Reinier III, Grace Kelly's husband, was the grandson of Juliette Louvet, a divorced cabaret singer, mother of two, and hostess at the Moulin Rouge of Toulouse-Lautrec fame. Juliette, being attractive and still young, did everything she could to support her two offsprings as a single mother, and in doing so met Prince Louis II of Monaco and became her lover. He fell in love with her and Juliette gave birth to their illegitimate daughter, Charlotte, in Algeria in 1898. Because the little girl was the prince's only child — mother and father never married — and Monaco needed an heir, the Prince gave her the surname Grimaldi. He also granted her the title of Duchess of Velentinois, for life. Charlotte eventually got married to Count Pierre de Polignac and had two children. One of them, a boy named Rainier, later became Prince Reinier III who married Grace Kelly, the starlet of Hollywood fame.

13. I had been reading her books. On one of my trips to Spain, I stopped for a few days in Paris and visited her tomb to place a bouquet in her memory. I was surprised to see mine was not the only one there. No matter how scandalous her life had been, Colette was the first French woman who was given a state funeral. It was also interesting to see that no cross appears on her tomb. I later learned that, because she had been divorced twice, she couldn't receive the last sacraments. According to her daughter, her mother had never wanted children, so the little girl was raised by an English nanny. Later, as she grew up, her mother didn't have a loving relationship with her. Even though they were never close, due to a twist of fate she and her daughter are buried side by side at Pere-Lachaise cemetery in Paris. So ironic, distant during their lifetime, they will be together throughout eternity. Putting aside her talent, the writer's behavior reminded me of Picasso and the indifference with which he also treated his children. Of course, this has nothing to do with being artistic or talented; however, not all artists behave this way.

14. Also known as the Marquise de Belbeuf, Mathilde de Morny was a masculine lesbian — always dressed as a man — who came from minor nobility and worked as a sculptor. In the sketch, Colette and Mathilde kissed, causing a major scandal where the police was involved. The Moulin Rouge was threatened with closure and

Mathilde lost her inheritance. The two lived together for six years. Mathilde committed suicide during the German occupation of Paris in 1944.

15. The museum became a reality later and I was able to visit it on another trip.

16. The city of Paris has other vineyards tucked in hilly areas. They include the one at Butte Bergeyre, Clos de Bercy, Clos de Morillon, and Clos Belleville.

17. It was never Picasso's intention to label the painting "*The Ladies*..." He called it "my brothel", for he used a house of ill fame, at Carrer d'Avinyó in Barcelona, for inspiration. But the probity of the times prevailed.

I was later thrilled to discover that Cuban painter and friend, Enrique Riverón [1902-1998], while studying in Paris on a scholarship, met Picasso. The Spanish great told him to "forget about the Academy and paint whatever you want." I visited Riverón often at his home in Coconut Grove (Miami). What Picasso said to him, he told me, was an awakening lesson.

Another Cuban who was there during the birth of modernism, Don Pedro Vidal de Solares y Cárdenas, shows up in Auguste Renoir's *Bal au Moulin de la Galette* (Mesée d'Orsay.) A friend of the famous impressionist painter, Don Pedro was a bon vivant bohemian and wannabe painter who could afford the Parisian lifestyle thanks to his family fortune. He's found dancing with the also famous Margot Legrand, a principal figure at the Moulin de la Galette.

18. Montmartre is still today a favorite for filmmakers like Woody Allen.

19. A friend of Cuban painter Enrique Riverón and her paramour, Swiss architect Le Corbusier.

20. Although mass communications outlets and universities have taken over the functions of the salon, I still think it is a pity we don't practice it anymore.

21. She was born in 1915 and died in 1963. At 4'-10", the diminutive Piaf was adored by the French, and everyone else. When she sang, her voice had a strange sound like a chirping bird, as if she had been wounded and was suffering. One of her songs, *La Vie en Rose*, from 1946, has been used in many movies. One that comes to mind is the motion picture Sabrina, filmed in 1954 with Audrey Hepburn as Sabrina, Humphrey Bogart as the conservative Linus, and William Holden as the immature David Larrabee.

22. *Sevillanas* have a set of worked-out steps. Different from Flamenco, which relies on improvisation, they are usually performed at fairs and private parties.

23. The second of its kind in Paris (1951). Owned by George Whitman and named *Le Mistral* and renamed (1964) *Shakespeare and Co.* as a tribute to Sylvia Beach. Sylvia was an American who opened her bookstore in Paris in 1919. S&C was where Hemingway, James Joyce, F. Scott Fitzgerald, Gertrude Stein and many other writers, who later became famous, gathered. The bookstore closed its doors by 1941 during the German occupation, when most writers dispersed to avoid the Nazis. Silvia and the store were featured in Hemingway's memoir, *A Moveable Feast*, and in Woody Allen's film, *Midnight in Paris*.

24. Although when he joined the first Impressionist exhibition his work did not fit the Impressionist mold, Cezanne, by 1875, brightened his palette and was convinced by Camille Pissarro to try it. The result was *Bathers* (1975). Always changing and experimenting, he began to distort his images (*Gardanne*) and, consequently, influenced (*The Card Players*) Post-Impressionism, Cubism and other avant-garde artists of the 20th Century.

25. Perhaps inspired by the Bon Bock (Good Pint) Society, a group with democratic ideals — after the Commune uprising was put down — that hosted monthly dinners in and around Montmartre.

26. Famous Parisian poet, writer and art critic who, more than anyone else, fought back with his pen those who criticized the new schools of painting being hatched, particularly in Montmartre and generally around France. Cubism — he coined the word — and Surrealism owe a lot to his writings. Wounded in WWI, he died at the age of 38 in the flu pandemic of 1918.

27. At 14 Escudellers Street, *Los Caracoles* is one of the most representative of the restaurants in Barcelona. A fixture at the same location since 1835, it's a flagship that illustrates the "feel" of *Ciutat Vella* (Old City) and specializes in the cuisine of Barcelona — anything from the sea is excellent. It has been in the hands of the Bofarull family for five generations.

28. The project took many years to complete. The construction costs, estimated at 7 million francs, were drawn from private donations, but it wasn't enough. Thus, pilgrimage donations quickly became the mainstay of the funding. The church architecture was inspired by the Romano-Byzantine style and designed by architect Paul Abadie. But he died after the foundation had been laid in 1884. Five architects continued with the work and the church was finally completed by 1914; however, it was formally dedicated in 1919, after WWI.

29. Although many years have passed, whenever I go to Spain we get together. She is now married with four handsome and well-behaved kids.

30. One was a 1988 film, *Camille Claudel*, starring Isabelle Adjani and Gerard Depardieu — a must-see. Also, *Camille Claudel 1915*, starring Juliette Binoche, filmed in 2013.

31. Known as the "Sun King", Louis holds the record for the longest tenure of any European monarch (elevated at age five); however, his influence in the development of the absolute head of state in France ended with the French Revolution. A warmonger, he used the short periods of peacetime to prepare for the next war. He also reversed religious freedom, forcing protestant minorities into exile.

32. No, nothing of nothing/No, I don't regret anything/Neither the good things people have done to me/Nor the bad things/It's all the same to me/No, nothing of nothing/No! I don't regret anything/It's paid for, swept away, forgotten/I don't care about the past!...

33. Miller (1891-1980) moved to Paris in 1930 and met Nin there. He left France when war broke out in 1939. Nin left in 1940.

34. Margaux and I had talked about Leslie Caron. They had met when Margaux and her husband were invited to a dinner at the American Embassy. She told me she now sees her often when Ms. Caron walks her Shih Tzu in the Tuileries garden, where Margaux also walks her peach-colored, well-behaved, poodle.

35. Located 400 feet from her museum, the childhood home of the woman who wrote "men are impossible" and then added "women too", has been opened since 2016.

36. There are two films about Vincent's life. I enjoyed both, *Lust for Life*, and *Vincent and Theo*.

37. Based on this painting, singer and songwriter, Don McLean, contributed with the song, *Vincent*, to the immortality of Van Gogh.

38. Some experts give credence to other paintings as Van Gogh's "last." *Tree Roots and Trunks* is one of them. A recent book, *Van Gogh: New Findings*, promotes this idea. In all likelihood, we will never know.

39. This quote is attributed to Henry of Navarre (Henry IV of France [1553-1610]). Knowing the French would never accept a Protestant king, he converted to Catholicism to save France, thus becoming a traitor to the Huguenots. Eventually, about a decade later, he issued the Edit of Nantes that granted Protestants the freedom to worship publicly.

THE EXHIBITION

Paris: Poetic Images of Night and Dawn

The Art of Nilda Cepero
March 9-31
French Heritage Month

Le Tour de France. Notre Dame

Light of Paris. Notre Dame

Lilac Mist. Montmartre

Looking in. Paris

175

Marie Antoinette Blues. Conciergerie

Memories Blue. Notre-Dame. The poet reading a love letter

Moon over Sacred Heart

Moon over Seine

Notre Dame in Purple

Once Upon a Time

Rooftops of Paris Blue

Rooftops in Purple

Silhouette of Rooftops. Paris

The Love Letter. Notre Dame

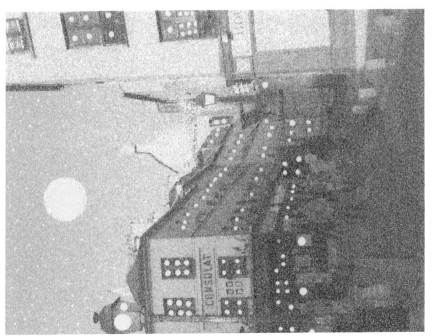

Village Blue. Montmartre

Writers Rendezvous

Crescent Moon at Place de Vosges

Across Time Final

Crescent Moon. Sacred Heart

Dawn. Pont Alexandre III

Daybreak Alexandre III Bridge

Elegance in Blue

Eternal Flame

Inner Drama in Purple. Paris

Evoking Lautrec

Final destination

Final Destination. Pantheon

From the Balcony. Le Marais

Girl on Bike. Place des Vosges

In-Flight. Notre Dame

Evening in Paris

Inner Drama. Notre Dame

Exhibición Fotográfica de Nilda Cepero

Desde el día nueve de marzo y hasta el final de dicho mes, se estará presentando en la Alianza Francesa, auspiciada por esa institución, la notable obra fotográfica de la artista del lente y escritora Nilda Cepero.

La Lic. Cepero, que estudió Historia Universal e Historia del Arte, es graduada de la Universidad Internacional de la Florida. También ha transitado por diferentes disciplinas como teatro y canto. Y siendo aficionada a la fotografía, su pasión la ha llevado a documentar a través de este medio sus raíces y sus viajes.

El título de esta exhibición, es "Viajes personales: París, Noche y Alborada".

El día de la inauguración se ofrecerá un cóctel que es por invitación, el viernes nueve de marzo a las 7:00 p.m. Lugar: En la Alianza Francesa 1414 Coral Way, Miami. La entrada es gratis.

TRANSLATION

From the 9th of March to the end of the month, the French Alliance is presenting and sponsoring the outstanding photographic work of the artist of the lens and writer, Nilda Cepero. A history major at Florida International University, she also completed graduate work in art history at the same institution, in addition to theater and vocal training. As an amateur, she has enjoyed photography and documented her travels. The title of this exhibition is Paris: Poetic Images of Night and Dawn. *On the first day of the exhibition there will be hors d'oeuvres and wine. Friday, starting at 7:00 PM. Venue: French Alliance 1414 Coral Way, Miami. Free.*

It was a privilege to be invited to Nilda's *Paris: Poetic Images of Night and Dawn* at the French Alliance. It was also a pleasure to be there with her; and, as it's sometimes said, "anybody who is anybody in the art world in South Florida", was there. My friend, at all times friendly and warm, invariably has always something new to share: A book of poetry; short stories; memoirs; a music CD where she offers, in her own voice, Cuban boleros. But this new phase as a photographer surprised me. Nilda has added a new dimension to her artistic life, and it is something that must be experienced with all senses. In each image one discovers, and it makes us aware, of this latest aspect of her special world. While there I enjoyed visually-stunning photographs. But, aside from the superb photos she also did an excellent job of framing, hanging, and lighting the show. My mother, who was French, would have loved the photographs as much as I did.

The gallery was full, as folks were commenting and eyeing the pictures and discussing them with their friends. They seemed intrigued and stimulated by her offering.

Nilda presents us with the beauty of Paris in marvelous, brilliant colors which made everyone there depart the French Alliance with a renewed sense of how Paris looks through this artist's eyes.

José Sánchez-Boudy
Diario Las Américas

From *The Miami New Times*

The author and Danielle Ferré-Culas, Associate Director, Alliance Française

WE'LL ALWAYS HAVE PARIS

Quick: Name three things about Paris that don't include the words "socialite," "blonde," or "stupid-rich." Well done, if you said anything like "home of the crêpe, the Louvre, and the fashionable beret." Shame on you if you said, "That's hot." Redeem yourself

Cherchez l'ambiance

tonight at an exhibit based on the only Paris worth mentioning, just in time for **French Heritage Month**. At 7:00 p.m. the Alliance Française of Miami presents the photography of Nilda Cepero. Cepero is a celebrated writer, editor, and poet, but tonight she'll be showing a collection of photos that pay homage to the City of Lights. The exhibit, **"Paris: Poetic Images of Night and Dawn,"** will run until March 31, but for tonight only, Cepero will be there to meet, greet, and school you. The wine tasting during the event will help to shake off those nerves. Drink and be merry at Alliance Française, 1414 Coral Way, Coral Gables. Admission is free. Call 305-859-8760, or visit www.afmiami.org.

RAINA McLEOD

Frank Fernández, author

Gabriel Casanova and Maucha Gutiérrez, radio personalities

Miguel Nin, painter

The sculptor Tony López and wife, Esperanza

Philippe Timon, Director,
Alliance Française [Miami]

Emilio Guerra, Professor and Sommelier

Author Juan Cueto and the flowers he sent while travelling in Egypt

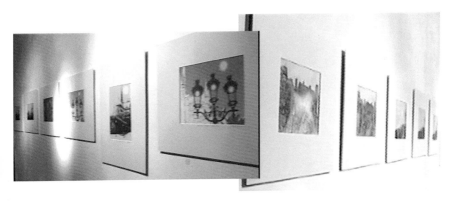

Rogelio Rodríguez and wife Simone, ballet teachers. Also, chorographers at the Moulin Rouge, Paris

Julio Gómez, Theater Director

Félix Pérez, Accountant

Ofelia Tavares
President, Cuban Museum

Miguel Saavedra
political activist

Luis González-Cruz, author

Julio Mata, author

María Díaz-Valenzuela, educator

Zilia Lage, author

Georges Ceada

ACKNOWLEDGEMENTS

Thanks to Clyde Aragón, a true friend from New Mexico who sends homemade cookies for me to enjoy. He was the first writer who dedicated a book to me. Also, special thanks to writer and artist, André Avellanet, who was always fun and loved Paris. He talked often about settling there after retirement. Sadly, Covid took him from us quite early. There is a lesson there for all of us.

Can forget the talented poet Alan Britt—cherished all his books—who has given me very good advice; Spanish novelist Juan Carlos Castillón who, from Barcelona, sends magnificent music for relaxation every week; enjoyable writer Juan Cueto-Roig, who makes me laugh with his hilarious emails; my dearest and marvelous writer-friend, Luis González-Cruz who, like me, loves to travel, and dared to sail around the world; the sublime poet and writer Luis Marcelino Gómez, with whom I had lots of laughs; the fine writer, I. G. Montserrat, who loves yoga; the delightful and talented poet Maya Isla, beautiful inside and out; Radamés Morales, a multi-talented writer and Boricua friend; the energetic Carlos Rubio, who never stops writing and, to my enjoyment, has shared all his magnificent books; the extraordinary writer, poet and artist, Mireya Robles; writer and professor Jacobo Machover, who was born in Cuba but has lived in Paris almost all of his life—this tome won't teach him anything new, but I hope he likes it.

And last, but not least, I wish to remember Danielle Juliet and Damian Anthony—having DNA so similar to mine—whose compassion, empathy and ethical behavior I'm sure someday will be rewarded. I know life will help them attain the goals of anything they might set their mind to do. May the future always be gentle to them.